Discovering
ENGLISH COUNTY
REGIMENTS

Arthur Taylor

GW00598775

COVER: *A detail of 'The 14th Foot at Waikato Paa, New Zealand, 1863', by Orlando Norie. (Courtesy of the National Army Museum).*

Shire Publications Ltd

CONTENTS

Copyright © 1970 and 1987 by Arthur Taylor. ISBN 0 85263 708 X.
All rights reserved. Shire Publications Ltd, Cromwell House, Church Street, Princes Risborough, Aylesbury, Bucks HP17 9AJ, UK.

INTRODUCTION

It was a stroke of genius on the part of those High Persons who order the fortunes of the British soldier to link individual English infantry regiments with the English shires for recruiting purposes. Territorial arrangements were made for Scottish, Irish and Welsh regiments as well, but the County as an object and source of honest local loyalty is essentially an English thing, and indeed, England itself. Moreover, those unpretentious regiments of English foot soldiers, lacking in dash, but hard to move from positions which they had been set to hold, were the mainstay of a centuries-old military policy which generally aimed to hold the line against would-be conquerors and disturbers of the civilised order of things. Whatever this country's detractors within and without may hold to the contrary, this policy has worked for the good of the world as a whole. It is significant that the British soldier seldom shone on those occasions when he was sent off to serve doubtful causes: there is nothing dishonourable about any of the battle honours listed in this book.

Since 1881, and in some cases longer, the ties between English regiments and English counties have grown and prospered. In keeping with other books in the 'Discovering' series, this one seeks to guide the reader to the visible marks of these ties—the Colours laid up in churches, the memorials and statues, the regimental museums—in the hope that he or she will learn something of their spirit while they are still with us. Military customs and traditions in general have been dealt with in another book in the series, and references to it have been made where appropriate to avoid duplication. Entries are under county headings for better reference, and at the head of each stands a brief note giving the origin of the regiment in question and the establishment of the county connection. For the sake of space, two abbreviations are used—'Bn' for 'Battalion' and 'Regt' for 'Regiment'. Battle honours are given in italic at the foot of the entry to serve as a brief account of the regiment's history, and a list giving details of these appears at the end of the book.

Since the first edition of this book change has overtaken even the historic counties, and the unfortunate inhabitants of such bureaucratic fancies as Avon and Cumbria will find no reference to their Babylonian captivity. However, the opportunity to incorporate amendments to the text suggested by Regimental Secretaries has been gladly utilised so as to pay honour where it is justly due.

THE BEDFORDSHIRE & HERTFORDSHIRE REGIMENT

Raised in 1688 as Douglass's Regt, later the 16th Foot. Became the Bedfordshire Regt in 1809.

In 1782 the 16th was allotted Buckinghamshire as its recruiting county, hence one of its nicknames, 'The Old Bucks'. Another was 'The Peace-makers', supposedly because it was stationed in Canada at the time of Waterloo, and arrived in Europe only to participate in the triumphal entry into Paris. By then, it had exchanged titles with the 14th Bedfordshire Regiment. To commemorate the many Hertfordshire men who served in it during the First World War, 'Hertfordshire' was added in 1919.

The Regiment wore white facings in full dress, and its march was *Mandolinata*. In 1958 it was amalgamated with The Essex Regiment to form what is now the 3rd Battalion, Royal Anglian Regiment. The regimental collection is housed in Luton Museum, Wardown Park, Luton. In 1980 the county designation was restored to the Battalion's title.

The majority of the Regiment's retired Colours are laid up in St. Paul's Church, Bedford. Others are lodged in the chapel of the old depot, the Church of the Transfiguration, Kempston, in St. Albans Cathedral, St. Mary's Church in Luton, and in the chapel of the new regiment at Warley, Brentwood.

In Bedford's High Street, a statue of a soldier of the 16th stands in memory of those who fell in the Boer War, depicting the uniform worn in that campaign. The memorial of the two World Wars is at Kempston, and in the church of St. Peter-upon-Cornhill, London, a window commemorates all ranks who fell in the service of the 16th from 1688 onwards.

Namur 1695, Blenheim, Ramillies, Oudenarde, Malplaquet, Surinam, Chitral, South Africa 1900-02.

Mons, Marne 1914, Ypres 1914 '15 '17, Loos, Somme 1916 '18, Arras 1917 '18, Cambrai 1917 '18, Sambre, Suvla, Gaza.

Dunkirk 1940, North West Europe 1940, Tobruk Sortie, Belhamed, Tunis, North Africa 1941 '43, Cassino II, Trasimine Line, Italy 1944-5, Chindits 1944.

4

THE ROYAL BERKSHIRE REGIMENT (PRINCESS CHARLOTTE OF WALES'S)

49th Foot raised in 1744 as Trelawney's Regt. 66th Foot, raised in 1755, became the Berkshire Regt in 1782. Linked as 1st and 2nd Bns in 1881.

In 1782, the 49th was designated the Hertfordshire Regiment and served on board ships of the Royal Navy as marines at the battle of Copenhagen in 1801. The officers' badge of the Berkshires was the dragon encircled by a coiled naval rope in commemoration of the episode. Princess Charlotte of Wales was so impressed by the 49th, that it was granted her title in 1815 at her request, and it went on to collect other honours—the Chinese dragon badge for service in the 'opium war' of 1839-42, and the 'Royal' title for the whole Regiment in 1885 for gallantry at the battle of Tofrek in the Sudan, when it was the 1st Battalion, The Berkshire Regiment.

As a royal regiment, it wore blue facings. Its march was *The Dashing White Sergeant.* Forbury Gardens in Reading contains a memorial to men of the 66th who fell in action at Maiwand, in 1880. Other memorials and retired Colours are in St. Mary's, St. George's and St. Laurence's churches in Reading; St. Michael's, Wallingford; St. Helen's Abingdon; Windsor Castle, and Osborne House, Isle of Wight.

In 1959, the Berkshires amalgamated with the Wiltshires as The Duke of Edinburgh's Royal Regiment (Berkshire and Wiltshire), which includes the dragon and naval rope in its badge. The museum is now in The Wardrobe, 58 The Close, Salisbury.

St. Lucia 1778, Egmont-op-Zee, Copenhagen, Duoro, Talavara, Albuhera, Queenstown, Vittoria, Pyrenees, Nivelle, Nive, Orthes, Peninsula, Alma, Inkerman, Sevastopol, Kandahar 1880, Afghanistan 1879-80, Egypt 1882, Tofrek, Suakin 1885, South Africa 1899-1902.
Mons 1914, Ypres 1914 '18, Neuve Chapelle, Loos, Somme 1916 '18, Arras 1917 '18, Cambrai 1917, Selle, Vittorio Veneto, Doiran 1917 '18.
Dyle, Dunkirk 1940, Normandy Landing, Rhine, Sicily 1943, Damiano, Anzio, Kohima, Mandalay, Burma 1942-5.

THE BUCKINGHAMSHIRE BATTALION, THE OXFORDSHIRE & BUCKINGHAMSHIRE LIGHT INFANTRY (T.A.)

Raised in 1859 as the Buckinghamshire Rifle Volunteer Corps.

This county once had two regular regiments of its own. The 16th Foot took the county title in 1782, but exchanged with the 14th or Bedfordshire Regiment in 1809 at the wish of the latter's Colonel, Sir Harry Calvert, who had estates in Buckinghamshire. The 14th gained many men from its new county during the rest of the war against Napoleon, but afterwards the connection was in name only. It became the West Yorkshire Regiment in 1881. Another regiment, the 85th Foot, was raised in the Aylesbury and Buckingham areas in 1793, and was known as the Bucks Volunteers until it became the 2nd Battalion, King's Shropshire Light Infantry in 1881.

After that, the county was in the recruiting area of the Oxfordshire Light Infantry. Pressure of local feeling caused this regiment to take 'Buckinghamshire' into its title in 1908.

The amateur soldiers of the Rifle Volunteers were attached to the Oxfordshires for training, but they resisted all official attempts to persuade them to trade their distinctive dark grey rifleman's uniform and busby for the scarlet of the regulars. They also preferred to be known as 'The Buckinghamshire Battalion', rather than the 4th Battalion, Oxfordshire and Buckinghamshire Light Infantry, and to keep their own march —*I'm Ninety-Five*, (originally the march of The Rifle Brigade, the 95th Foot).

The Battalion had no separate battle honours, but shared those of the parent regiment. A company of volunteers went out to join the Oxfordshires in the Boer War, but the Battalion began its own fighting career in the First World War in France and Italy. During the Second, it distinguished itself by a gallant defence of Hazebrouck, south of Dunkirk. The position was finally overwhelmed, and only 200 survivors struggled back to England. The Battalion returned to France on D-Day.

It is now disbanded. There is a small memorial chapel in St. Mary's Church, Aylesbury. Some uniforms are displayed at the T.A. Centre, Oxford Road, Aylesbury and there are items in the Royal Green Jacket's Museum, Winchester.

THE CAMBRIDGESHIRE REGIMENT (T.A.)

Raised in 1860 as the Cambridgeshire Rifle Volunteers.

The 30th Foot was designated the Cambridgeshire Regiment in 1782, but when it became the 1st Battalion, The East Lancashire Regiment in 1881, the county was left without a regular regiment of its own. When the Territorial Force was organised in 1908, the local Rifle Volunteers became The Cambridgeshire Regiment, affiliated to the regular Suffolk Regiment for training.

They adopted the scarlet tunics and march of the Suffolks, *Speed the Plough,* but wore royal blue facings, a rare privilege for a non-royal regiment, shared only with the Somerset Light Infantry.

Two battalions were raised for the Second World War, and both were sent to the Far East when the Japanese struck at Malaya in December, 1941. With the rest of their division, the Cambridgeshire battalions were thrown into the battle with little preparation. Both fought gallantly in the desperate jungle battles, and were involved in the final disaster at Singapore. The survivors endured three and a half years of Japanese captivity. 760 members died in the fighting, or afterwards in the prison camps.

The Regiment took its drums to Singapore, and they were stored there when it went off to battle. The island fell and the drums were presumed lost. In 1945 they were found in a thicket in Malaya. It was decided that they should never be played again, but paraded with the Regiment in silence, in memory of the men who did not return.

There is regimental material in the Suffolk's museum, Gibraltar Barracks, Bury St. Edmunds and Ely Museum. Ely Cathedral holds the Colours. The Regiment is now disbanded but in 1980 the county title was added as a supplementary designation for the 1st Battalion, The Royal Anglian Regiment.

Ypres 1915 '17, Somme 1916 '18, Ancre Heights, Pilchem, Passchendaele, Kemmel, Amiens, Hindenburg Line, Pursuit to Mons, France & Flanders 1915-18.
Jahore, Batu-Pahat, Singapore Island, Malaya 1942.

THE 22nd (CHESHIRE) REGIMENT

Raised in 1689 as The Duke of Norfolk's Regiment. Became the Cheshire Regiment in 1782.

Tradition has it that this regiment won its oak-leaf badge at the battle of Dettingen in 1743, when some of its members defended King George II during a French attack. According to the tale, the grateful monarch plucked a leaf from the tree by which he was standing, and awarded it to their officer as a badge of honour. An alternative explanation is that a sprig of acorn appeared in the coat-of-arms of the regiment's first colonel, the Duke of Norfolk.

Certainly, the badge has long been worn in the 22nd. It is borne on the Regimental Colour, and in the presence of royalty and on special occasions, wreaths of oak-leaves are carried on the Colours and the oak-leaf is worn in the head-dress.

The 22nd wore buff facings in full dress. It has a number of marches, used for different occasions—*Come Lasses and Lads* provides an assembly march, *Young May Moon* (the old Regimental quick step), the slow march *The Duke of York, The Regimental March of the 22nd,* and others.

The retired Colours of the Regiment are laid up in Chester Cathedral. The museum is in Chester Castle, and contains uniforms, medals, weapons and pictures. Of particular interest is a diorama of the battle of Meeanee, 1843, where the 22nd was part of a small force under that great soldier, Sir Charles Napier, which won a victory over 30,000 Baluchis in India. The museum has relics of Napier himself, and the Regimental Chapel is in the same building.

Loiusburg, Martinique 1762, Havannah, Meeanee, Hyderabad, Scinde, South Africa 1900-02.

Mons, Ypres 1914 '15 '17 '18, Somme 1916 '18, Arras 1917 '18, Messines 1917 '18, Bapaume 1918, Doiran 1917 '18, Suvla, Gaza, Kut-al-Amara 1917.

St. Omer-la-Bassee, Normandy Landing, Capture of Tobruk, El Alamein, Mareth, Sicily 1943, Salerno, Rome, Gothic Line, Malta 1941-2.

8

THE DUKE OF CORNWALL'S LIGHT INFANTRY

32nd Foot raised in 1702 as Fox's Marines. Became the Cornwall Regt in 1782. 46th Foot raised in 1741 as Price's Regt. Linked as 1st and 2nd Bns in 1881.

The 32nd was designated a light infantry regiment in 1858 to honour its gallant defence of Lucknow during the Indian Mutiny. The siege lasted for 140 days, and for 87 of them the regiment was alone.

The 46th became the South Devonshire Regiment in 1782. During the American rebellion, light companies from several regiments including the 46th surprised an American camp at Paoli, inflicting heavy casualties. The colonists vowed vengeance, and the British sent word that they would dye their cap feathers red, so that the Americans would not mistake them. The light company of the 46th always wore red feathers after that, and eventually the whole regiment. In modern times, they were represented by a red cloth backing to the cap badge.

The two regiments were linked as The Duke of Cornwall's Light Infantry, which wore white facings. The regimental march was a combination of *One and all* and *Trelawny*. The museum is in the Keep, Bodmin Barracks, before which stands a statue of a soldier in the fighting kit of the First World War, the war memorial. St. Petroc's Church in the town contains other memorials and the Colours. In 1959, the D.C.L.I. was amalgamated with the Somerset Light Infantry to form what has been since 1968 the 1st Battalion, The Light Infantry.

Gibraltar 1704-5, Dettingen, St. Lucia 1778, Dominica, Rolica, Vimiera, Corunna, Salamanca, Pyrenees, Nivelle, Nive, Orthes, Peninsula, Waterloo, Mooltjan, Goojerat, Punjaub, Sevastapol, Lucknow, Tel-el-Kebir, Egypt 1882, Nile 1884-5, Paardeberg, South Africa 1899-1902.

Mons, Marne 1914, Ypres 1915' 17, Somme 1916 '18, Arras 1917, Passchendaele, Cambrai 1917 '18, Sambre, Doiran 1917 '18, Gaza.

Hill 112, Mont Pincon, Nederrijn, Geilenkirchen, Rhineland, North West Europe 1940, 1944-5, Gazala, Medjez Plain, Cassino II, Incentro.

THE BORDER REGIMENT

34th Foot raised in 1702 as Lucas's Regt. 55th Foot raised in 1757.

In 1782, the 34th Foot became the Cumberland Regiment, and the 55th the Westmorland Regiment. They were linked in 1881 as The Border Regiment. Its march was, of course, *John Peel,* and in full dress it wore yellow facings.

At the battle of Arroyo dos Molinos in Spain, during the Napoleonic War, the 34th captured the French 34th Regiment and its drums. Annually, the English 34th celebrated this event by parading the captured drums.

On the Regimental Colour and the cap badge of The Border Regiment appeared the Chinese dragon awarded to the 55th for its service in the 'opium war' of 1840-42.

In the Second World War, the 1st Battalion became part of the 1st Airborne Division, and were subsequently the first British soldiers to go into a major action by glider, this during the 1943 invasion of Sicily. For this the Regiment was granted the right to wear on its right sleeves a glider badge. This right is still exercised by the King's Own Royal Border Regiment, the new regiment formed in 1959 by the amalgamation of The Border Regiment with The King's Own Royal Regiment (Lancaster).

The museum is in Queen Mary's Tower, Carlisle Castle, and its Colours are in the Regimental Chapel in Carlisle Cathedral.

Havannah, St. Lucia 1778, Albuhera, Arroyo dos Molinos, Vittoria, Pyrenees, Nivelle, Nive, Orthes, Peninsula, Alma, Inkerman, Sevastopol, Lucknow, Relief of Ladysmith, South Africa 1899-1902, Afghanistan 1919.

Ypres 1914 '15 '17 '18, Langemarck 1914 '17, Somme 1916 '18, Arras 1917 '18, Cambrai 1917 '18, Lys, France & Flanders 1914-18, Vittorio Veneto, Macedonia 1915-18, Gallipoli 1915-16.

Dunkirk 1940, Arnhem 1944, North West Europe 1940 '44, Tobruk 1941, Landing in Sicily, Imphal, Myinmu Bridgehead, Meiktila, Chindits 1944, Burma 1943-5.

THE SHERWOOD FORESTERS (NOTTINGHAMSHIRE & DERBYSHIRE REGIMENT)

95th Foot raised in 1823, becoming the Derbyshire Regt in 1825, and 2nd Bn The Sherwood Foresters (Derbyshire Regt) in 1881.

The 95th's first taste of serious fighting came in the Crimean War. At the battle of Alma, it captured a set of Russian drums, and to commemorate the battle the Foresters' drums had edges painted with black and white triangles in the Russian fashion. In the same action, casualties were so heavy among the Colour party that one of the Colours had to be carried by an ordinary soldier. On the annual celebration of Alma Day it was the custom to entrust one of the Colours to the longest serving soldier.

Campaigning in the Indian Mutiny soon after, the 95th 'liberated' a fighting ram tethered in a temple yard. It remained with them during six fights, and as 'Private Derby' was awarded the India Medal. The 95th kept a ram as a mascot thereafter, which appeared on parade in its Regimental coat and led by its orderlies in full dress.

The hart in the centre of the Regimental badge was derived from the arms of Derby and has been perpetuated in the badge of the amalgamated regiment which was formed in 1970. A beacon tower with the Forester's badge above the door forms the war memorial on the summit of Crich hill in the county.

The main museum is in Nottingham Castle but there is some material in the civic museum in the Strand, Derby.

Louisburg, Rolica, Vimiera, Talavura, Busaco, Fuentes d'Onor, Cuidad Rodrigo, Badajoz, Salamanca, Vittoria, Pyrenees, Nivelle, Orthes, Toulouse, Peninsula, Ava, South Africa 1846-7, Alma, Inkerman, Sevastopol, Central India, Abyssinia, Egypt 1882, Tirah, South Africa 1899-1902.

Aisne 1914 '18, Neuve Chapelle, Loos, Somme 1916 '18, Ypres 1917 '18, Cambrai 1917 '18, St. Quentin Canal, France & Flanders 1914-18, Italy 1917-18, Gallipoli 1915.

Norway 1940, Gazala, El Alamein, Tunis, Salerno, Anzio, Campoleone, Gothic Line, Coriano, Singapore Island.

THE DEVONSHIRE REGIMENT

11th Foot raised in 1685 as the Duke of Beaufort's Regt. Became the North Devonshire Regt in 1782.

The Devons received their final title in 1881. The nickname 'The Bloody Eleventh' was earned in the battle of Salamanca, 1808. After fierce fighting, the regiment took a leading part in the capture of the last French position, but was itself reduced to seventy men. Another epic of military history is the stand of the 2nd Battalion at Bois de Buttes, during the German drive on Paris in 1918. Ordered to defend their important position to the last, they did so quite literally, until there were only seven men left, all of whom were wounded. For this the battalion was awarded the French Croix de Guerre.

The Devons wore Lincoln green facings, and their badge included a representation of Exeter Castle. Their marches were *We've lived and loved together,* which was a popular air at the time of Salamanca, and the old Devonshire song *Widdecombe Fair.* In 1958 the Regiment was amalgamated with the neighbouring Dorset Regiment to form The Devonshire and Dorset Regiment and Exeter's castle and motto appear on the new badge.

The museum is in Wyvern Barracks, Topsham Road, Exeter, with material for the amalgamated regiment in The Keep, Dorchester. The Regimental Chapel is in Exeter Cathedral, and contains a very striking bronze statue of a First World War rifleman at bay, as well as the old Colours.

Dettingen, Salamanca, Pyrenees, Nivelle, Nive, Orthes, Toulouse, Peninsula, Afghanistan 1879-80, Tirah, Defence of Ladysmith, Relief of Ladysmith, South Africa 1899-1902.

La Bassee 1914, Ypres 1915 '17, Loos, Somme 1916 '18, Bois de Buttes, Hindenburg Line, Vittorio Veneto, Doiran 1917 '18, Palestine 1917-18, Mesopotamia 1916-18.

Normandy Landing, Caen, Rhine, North West Europe 1944-45, Landing in Sicily, Regalbuto, Malta 1940-42, Imphal, Myinmu Bridgehead, Burma 1943-45.

THE DORSET REGIMENT

39th Foot raised in 1702 as Coote's Regt, becoming the Dorsetshire Regt in 1807. 54th Foot raised in 1755. Linked as 1st and 2nd Bns in 1881.

The badge of the Dorsets included the motto *Primus in Indis,* marking the fact that the 39th was the first British regiment to serve in India. The castle and key stood for its part in the defence of Gibraltar during the siege of 1779-83. The sphinx was the 54th's badge. During the campaign against the French in Egypt in 1801, the regiment captured Fort Marabout, which commanded the entrance to Alexandra harbour. Until 1840, the 54th had the privilege of parading with one of the captured guns, but it was withdrawn in that year, and the battle honour 'Marabout' awarded instead. This was possessed only by the 54th; they were the the West Norfolks from 1782, until they became the 2nd Dorsetshires in 1881.

The Dorsets wore grass-green facings in full dress, and marched to *The Maid of Glenconnel,* and *The Farmer's Boy.* The museum, which numbers among its fine exhibits the Marabout gun, is in The Keep, Dorchester, and the Borough Gardens have a memorial to those of the Regiment who fell at Tirah. 37 Colours are lodged in Sherborne Abbey, which holds the Regimental Chapel. Beds have been endowed in the Dorset County Hospital and a tablet placed there in memory of Dorsets killed in 1914-18, and in Dorchester, Sherborne and Upton there are memorial houses, distinguished by the regimental badge carved on their fronts. The new badge of the amalgamated Devons and Dorsets carries the India motto and the sphinx.

Plassey, Martinique, Marabout, Albuhera, Vittoria, Pyrenees, Nivelle, Nive, Orthes, Peninsula, Ava, Maharajpore, Sevastopol, Tirah, Relief of Ladysmith, South Africa 1899-1902.

Mons, Marne 1914, Ypres 1915 '17, Somme 1916 '18, Hindenburg Line, Sambre, Suvla, Gaza, Shaiba, Ctesiphon.

St. Omer-la-Bassee, Normandy Landing, Caen, Arnhem 1944, Aam, Geilenkirchen, Landing in Sicily, Malta 1940-42, Kohima, Mandalay.

THE DURHAM LIGHT INFANTRY

68th Foot raised in 1856, became the Durham Regt in 1782.

The 'Faithful Durhams' spent much of their early service in the disease-ridden West Indies, and it was for this unglamorous colonial service that they earned their nickname. In 1808 the 68th was selected for training as a crack light infantry corps, and wore the honoured bugle-horn badge thereafter.

The 2nd Battalion began its life in India as the 2nd Bombay European Light Infantry, in the private army of the Honourable East India Company. When the Company was abolished in 1858 and its commitments in India were taken over by the British government, its European regiments were taken into the British army. This one became the 106th Light Infantry, and a battalion of the Durham Light Infantry in 1881.

The D.L.I. wore dark green facings. Its quick march was *The Light Barque* and its slow march *The Old 68th*. Being light infantry, however, the Durhams doubled past the saluting base on ceremonial occasions to *The Keel Row,* and *Moneymusk*, tunes which are the cavalry 'Trot Past'.

In 1968, the D.L.I. merged its identity with the new 'large' regiment, The Light Infantry.

The Durhams' Colours are laid up in Durham Cathedral and in the parish church of Barnard Castle. There is also a memorial garden in the cathedral close. The museum is housed in the Arts Centre, Ayley Heads, Durham.

Salamanca, Vittoria, Pyrenees, Nivelle, Orthes, Peninsula, Alma, Inkerman, Sevastopol, Reshire, Bushire, Koosh-ab, Persia, New Zealand, Relief of Ladysmith, South Africa 1899-1902, Afghanistan 1919.
Aisne 1914 '18, Ypres 1915 '17 '18, Hooge 1915, Loos, Somme 1916 '18, Arras 1917 '18, Messines 1917, Lys, Hindenburg Line, Sambre.
Dunkirk 1940, Tilly-sur-Seulles, Defence of Rauray, Gheel, Tobruk 1941, El Alamein, Mareth, Primosole Bridge, Salerno, Kohima, Korea 1952-3.

THE ESSEX REGIMENT

44th Foot raised in 1741; 56th Foot in 1755. They became the East Essex and West Essex Regts in 1782 and were linked as 1st and 2nd Bns in 1881.

The castle and key badge was awarded to the 56th for the defence of Gibraltar in the siege of 1779-83. The sphinx was won for service in Egypt in 1801 by the 44th, which also captured the Eagle of the French 62nd Regiment at Salamanca in 1812, commemorated by the eagle collar badges afterwards worn by Essex officers. Under the SOMERSET entry will be found the story of the massacre of the Kabul garrison in 1841; the 44th was the only British regiment in that unhappy force. Twenty men made a last stand at Gundamak, and the remnants of their Regimental Colour hang in the Chapel, having been wrapped around the body of an officer whose life was spared.

The Essex wore purple facings, and its march was *The Hampshires*. On St. Patrick's Day, the Corps of Drums used to beat reveille by playing Irish airs to mark the brief life of the 2nd Battalion of the 44th. It was raised in Ireland in 1803, won four of the Regiment's battle honours and captured the Eagle before it was disbanded at the end of the war.

The Regimental Chapel is at Eagle Way, Warley, Brentwood, and contains the Colours and the captured Eagle. Colours are also laid up in Colchester and in Chelmsford where there is a regimental memorial in obelisk form. The museum is in the Chelmsford and Essex Museum, Moulsham Street, Chelmsford.

In 1958 the Essex amalgamated with the Bedfordshires and Hertfordshires and in 1980 recovered the county designation as a supplementary Battalion title.

Moro, Havannah, Badajoz, Salamanca, Peninsula, Bladensburg, Waterloo, Ava, Alma, Inkerman, Sevastopol, Taku Forts, Nile 1884-5, Relief of Kimberley, Paardeberg, South Africa 1889-1902.

Le Cateau, Marne 1914, Ypres 1915 '17, Loos, Somme 1916 '18, Arras 1917 '18, Cambrai 1917 '18, Selle, Gallipoli 1915-16, Gaza. Zetten, North West Europe 1940, 1944-5, Palmyra, Tobruk 1941, Defence of Alamein Line, Enfidaville, Sangro, Villa Grande, Casino I, Chindits 1944.

THE GLOUCESTERSHIRE REGIMENT

28th Foot raised in 1694 as Gibson's Regt; 61st Foot raised in 1756. They became the North and South Gloucestershire Regts in 1782, 1st and 2nd Bns in 1881.

At Alexandria in 1801, the 28th was hotly engaged by French attacks on its front, when it was charged in the rear by cavalry. On the command, the rear rank faced about and dealt with the new assailants, then turned back to the main battle. For this, the 28th was given the unique privilege of wearing its number on the back as well as the front of its headdress. The 61st fought in the same campaign, and both were awarded the sphinx badge. When the two were linked as The Gloucestershire Regiment, the problem of the 'back number' was solved by both battalions adopting a 'back badge', a sphinx encircled by a laurel wreath.

The Gloucestershires' facings are primrose yellow, and their marches are *The Kinnegad Slashers* (28th) and *The Highland Piper* (61st). The museum is in the Custom House, 31 Commercial Road, Gloucester, and retired Colours are laid up in the Cathedral, in which is also the Celtic cross carved by Colonel Carne, V.C. in a Korean prison camp after the Imjin battle in 1951. A statue of a soldier of the Regiment in Boer War uniform is in Clifton.

Ramillies, Louisburg, Guadaloupe, 1759, Quebec 1759, Martinique 1762, Havannah, St. Lucia 1778, Maida, Corunna, Talavara, Busaco, Barrosa, Albuhera, Salamanca, Vittoria, Pyrenees, Nivelle, Nive, Orthes, Toulouse, Peninsula, Waterloo, Chillianwallah, Goojerat, Punjaub, Alma, Inkerman, Sevastopol, Delhi 1857, Defence of Ladysmith, Relief of Kimberley, Paardeberg, South Africa 1899-1902.

Mons, Ypres 1914 '15 '17, Loos, Somme 1916 '18, Lys, Selle, Vittorio Veneto, Doiran 1917, Sari Bair, Baghdad.

Defence of Escaut, Cassel, Mont Pincon, Falaise, North-West Europe 1940, 1944-5, Taukyan, Paungde, Pinwe, Myitson, Burma 1942 '44-5, Imjin, Korea 1950-1.

THE ROYAL HAMPSHIRE REGIMENT

37th Foot raised in 1702 as Meridith's Regt. 67th Foot raised in 1756. They became the North and South Hampshire Regts in 1782, the 1st and 2nd Bns in 1881.

The 37th was one of the six Minden regiments which attacked and routed French cavalry at the battle of Minden in 1759, due to a mistaken order. Afterwards, the survivors decked their hats with sweetbriars as tokens of victory. The 37th and the others celebrated the anniversary of the battle by Trooping their Colour, wearing roses in their headdress.

The Bengal tiger badge was awarded to the 67th by George III, for service in India from 1805 to 1826. The two regiments were linked as The Hampshire Regiment in 1881, which was granted the 'Royal' title in 1946.

The Hampshire 'Tigers' wear yellow facings. Their marches are *The Highland Piper* (37th) and *We'll gang nae mair to yon toon* (76th).

The museum is in Serle's House, Southgate Street, Winchester, which is the Regimental headquarters. The Colours of five of the Regiment's battalions are lodged there, and others are to be found in Portsmouth Cathedral, and St. Peter's Church, Bournemouth. There are memorial windows in Winchester Cathedral, the Garrison Church, Winchester, All Saints church, Aldershot, and the Chapel of the Royal Military Academy, Sandhurst.

Blenheim, Ramillies, Oudenarde, Malplaquet, Dettingen, Minden, Belleisle, Tournay, Barrosa, Peninsula, Taku Forts, Pekin 1860, Charasiah, Kabul 1879, Afghanistan 1878-80, Burma 1885-7, Paardeberg, South Africa 1900-02.

Retreat from Mons, Ypres 1915 '17 '18, Somme 1916 '18, Arras 1917 '18, Cambrai 1917 '18, Doiran 1917 '18, Landing at Helles, Suvla, Gaza, Kut al Amara 1915 '17.

Dunkirk 1940, Normandy Landing, Caen, Rhine, Tebourba Gap, Hunt's Gap, Salerno, Cassino II, Gothic Line, Malta 1941-2.

17

THE HEREFORDSHIRE LIGHT INFANTRY (T.A.)

The 36th Foot was designated the Herefordshire Regt between 1782 and 1881. In 1909 the title was given to the county's Territorial Bn, affiliated to the K.S.L.I.

With green facings in full dress, the Regiment marched to *The Lincolnshire Poacher*. In 1947 it became a Light Infantry regiment.

There are memorials in Hereford Cathedral, and museum items and Colours in the T.A. Centre, Harold Street, Hereford.

South Africa 1900-02, Soissonnais-Ourcq, Ypres 1918, Courtrai, France & Flanders 1918, Landing at Suvla, Rumani, Gaza, El Mughar, Jerusalem, Tell Asur.

Odon, Bourguebus Ridge, Souleuvre, Falaise, Antwerp, Hechtel, Venraij, Hochwald, Aller, North West Europe 1944-5.

HERTFORDSHIRE

THE HERTFORDSHIRE REGIMENT (T.A.)

Between 1782 and 1881, the 49th Foot was the Hertfordshire Regt. In 1909 the Bedfordshire Regt's local Territorial Bn took the title.

Brigaded with the Guards in the First World War, the 1st Bn was nicknamed 'The Herts Guards'. The Regiment wore white facings and its march was *The Young May Moon*. Colours and memorials are in All Saints', Hertford. The Hertford Museum displays some regimental material.

South Africa 1900-02.

Ypres 1914 '17, Festubert 1915, Loos, Somme 1916 '18, Ancre 1918, Pilckem, St. Quentin, Hindenburg Line, Sambre, France & Flanders 1914-18.

Normandy Landing, North West Europe 1944, Montorsoli, Gothic Line, Monte Gamberaldi, Monte Ceco, Monte Grande, Italy 1944-5.

HUNTINGDONSHIRE   *See under East Surrey Regiment.*

THE BUFFS (THE ROYAL EAST KENT REGIMENT)

Raised in 1572 for the Dutch service. Later became 3rd Foot, and the East Kent Regt in 1782.

This was the oldest regular regiment in the British army, but as it was not taken into the king's service until 1665 this did not show in the order of seniority. It was initially raised in London, so in due course was granted the privilege of marching through the City with 'drums beating, Colours flying, and bayonets fixed' . . . an honour sparingly given by a city with a long tradition of resistance to official displays of force.

The title of the Buffs came from the facing colour, but the origin of its dragon badge is not known, only that in 1751 it was officially confirmed as its 'ancient badge'.

The Buffs amalgamated with The Royal West Kents in 1961 to form The Queen's Own Buffs, and no longer wore the dragon badge, but it has reappeared in the cap badge of the new Queen's Regiment, the 'large regiment' formed in 1966 from regiments of the former Home Counties Brigade. The Queen's Own Buffs formed the 2nd Battalion.

The quick march of the old regiment was *The Buffs*, and its slow march was *Men of Kent*. There is a memorial in the Chapel of the Tower of London, but the Colours and other memorials are in the Warrior's Chapel in Canterbury Cathedral. A soldier enters the latter Chapel every day to turn a page in the Book of Remembrance. The museum is in The Royal Museum, High Street, Canterbury. The Queen's Regimental museum is in Dover Castle.

Blenheim, Ramillies, Oudenarde, Malplaquet, Dettingen, Guadaloup 1759, Belleisle, Duoro, Talvara, Albuhera, Vittoria, Pyrenees, Nivelle, Nive, Orthes, Toulouse, Peninsula, Punniar, Sevastopol, Taku Forts, South Africa 1879, Chitral, Relief of Kimberley, Paardeberg, South Africa 1900-02.

Armentières 1914, Ypres 1915 '17, Loos, Somme 1916 '18, Arras 1917, Amiens, Hindenburg Line, Struma, Jerusalem, Baghdad.

North West Europe 1940, Alem Hamza, El Alamein, Robaa Valley, Sicily 1943, Trigno, Anzio, Argenta Gap, Leros, Shweli.

THE QUEEN'S OWN ROYAL WEST KENT REGIMENT

50th Foot raised in 1756, becoming the West Kent Regt in 1782. 97th Foot raised in 1824. Linked as 1st and 2nd Bns in 1881.

The 50th was granted the title The Queen's Own in 1831. Until then it had worn black facings, which gave rise to the nickname 'The Dirty Half Hundred'. The nickname of the 97th was also derived from its facings. It was raised by the Earl of Ulster, and wore the blue of the ribbon of the Order of St. Patrick, which has been variously described as sky blue and heavenly blue. Hence the Regiment was known as 'The Celestials'.

The Royal West Kents wore royal blue facings, and the white horse badge of the ancient kingdom of Kent which also appears in the county's arms. The quick march was, surprisingly, *A Hundred Pipers,* and the slow march the more appropriate *Men of Kent.*

The Regiment's last battle honour was its finest. In 1944 the Japanese drive into India was checked at Kohima by the West Kents and two Indian battalions. Cut off, under fire night and day from all sides, driven on to a single hill, they held out for sixteen days, until relieved. Four thousand Japanese dead lay around the position.

As explained above, the Royal West Kents and The Buffs were amalgamated. The Colours are laid up in All Saints church, Maidstone. There is a cenotaph in Brenchly Gardens, and the museum is in Maidstone Museum, in St. Faith's Street.

Vimiera, Corunna, Almarez, Vittoria, Pyrenees, Nive, Orthes, Peninsula, Punniar, Moodkee, Ferozeshah, Aliwal, Sobroan, Alma, Inkerman, Sevastopol, Lucknow, New Zealand, Egypt 1882, Nile 1884-85, South Africa 1900-02, Afghanistan 1919.

Mons, Ypres 1914 '15 '17 '18, Hill 60, Somme 1916 '18, Vimy 1917, Italy 1917-18, Gallipoli 1915, Gaza, Defence of Kut al Amara, Sharqat.

North West Europe 1940, El Alamein, Medjez Plain, Centuripe, Sangro, Cassino, Trasimene Line, Argenta Gap, Malta 1940-2, Defence of Kohima.

THE KING'S OWN ROYAL REGIMENT (LANCASTER)

4th Foot raised in 1680 as the 2nd Tangier Regt. Designated the Royal Lancaster Regt in 1881.

This regiment was raised for the specific purpose of guarding Tangier in the first expansion of the small army of King Charles II. At the time, the very existence of a regular army was a highly suspect novelty in this country. Association with royalty began soon after, when the regiment received the title The Duchess of York and Albany's Regiment. In 1685, the Duke of York became King James II, and his consort's soldiers The Queen's.

The royal lion badge was granted by King William III, and the title The King's Own in 1715. The Regiment wore royal blue facings in full dress, and its march was *Corn Riggs are Bonny*. In 1959, it was amalgamated with The Border Regiment, and the King's Own Royal Border Regiment which resulted from this union wears the Royal Lion of England as its badge.

The museum of the new Regiment is in Queen Mary's Tower, The Castle, Carlisle. Most of the retired Colours and other memorials are in the Regimental Chapel in Priory Church, Lancaster, but the Colours carried by the 4th King's Regiment at the battle of Culloden in 1746 hang in Edinburgh Castle, side by side with those of the Appin Stewart clan against whom they fought. The museum of the King's Own is in the Old Town Hall, Market Square, Lancaster.

Namur 1695, Gibraltar 1704-5, Guadaloupe 1759, St. Lucia 1778, Corunna, Badajoz, Salamanca, Vittoria, San Sebastian, Nive, Peninsula, Bladensburg, Waterloo, Alma, Inkerman, Sevastopol, Abyssinia, South Africa 1879, Relief of Ladysmith, South Africa 1900-02.

Marne 1914, Ypres 1915 '17, Somme 1916 '18, Arras 1917 '18, Messines 1917, Lys, France & Flanders 1914-18, Macedonia 1915-18, Gallipoli 1915, Mesopotamia 1916-18.

Dunkirk 1940, North West Europe 1940, Defence of Habbaniya, Merjayun, Tobruk Sortie, North Africa 1940-2, Montone, Lamone Bridgehead, Malta 1941-2, Chindits 1944.

THE KING'S REGIMENT (LIVERPOOL)

8th Foot raised in 1685 as Princess Anne of Denmark's Regt. Became The Liverpool Regt in 1881.

In 1702, Princess Anne became Queen of England, and the title of the regiment was accordingly changed to The Queen's. With the accession of the German Elector of Hanover as King George I in 1715, the title was changed again to The King's, which it has remained to this day.

The badge is therefore very appropriate: the White Horse of Hanover. In the eighteenth century, in deference to George I and his successors, the grenadiers of every regiment in the English army bore the Hanover horse on their caps. The Queen's Own Hussars and The Prince of Wales' Own Regiment of Yorkshire wear it still. The King's wore blue facings, and its marches were *Here's to the Maiden, Zachmi Dill* and *The English Rose.*

The museum has been established in the Merseyside County Museums in William Brown Street, Liverpool. A memorial to the men of the Regiment who fell in the colonial wars of the nineteenth century is opposite the museum. It consists of bronze figures of soldiers wearing the uniforms of 1685, the eighteenth century and the South African War. Another memorial for the Indian Mutiny is in Whitley Gardens, Shaw Street, and the Colours and books of remembrance are lodged in the Anglican Cathedral. One Colour is in Salisbury Cathedral. In 1958 the King's amalgamated with The Manchester Regiment to form The King's Regiment (Manchester and Liverpool), whose badge includes the Hanover horse. The City designations were omitted from the Regiment's title in 1969.

Blenheim, Ramillies, Oudenarde, Malplaquet, Dettingen, Martinique 1809, Niagara, Delhi 1857, Lucknow, Peiwar Kotal, Afghanistan 1878-80, Burma 1885-7, Defence of Ladysmith, South Africa 1899-1902. Afghanistan 1919.

Retreat from Mons, Marne 1914, Aisne 1914, Ypres 1914 '15 '17, Festubert 1915, Loos, Somme 1916 '18, Arras 1917 '18, Scarpe 1917 '18, Cambrai 1917 '18.

Normandy Landing, Cassino II, Transimine Line, Tuori, Capture of Forli, Rimini Line, Athens, Chindits 1943, Chindits 1944, Korea 1952-53, The Hook 1953.

THE LANCASHIRE FUSILIERS

20th Foot raised in 1688 as Peyton's Regt. Became the Lancashire Fusiliers in 1881.

This was another of the Minden regiments (see page 17) but in addition, the 20th celebrated 'Gallipoli Day' annually to mark the 1915 landings. It possessed the ship's bell of H.M.S. *Euryalus* which carried the fusiliers to that ill-fated place, and used it to sound the time in barracks.

The full dress was a racoon-skin fusilier cap with a yellow hackle, and scarlet tunic with white facings. The old custom of heading ceremonial parades with pioneers wearing buck-skin aprons and gauntlets and carrying axes was maintained, and the Regiment marched to *The British Grenadiers* and *The Minden March*.

The museum is at Wellington Barracks in Bury, and the Colours and other memorials are in St. Mary's church. Outside the barracks is the 1914-18 War memorial, in the form of an obelisk flanked by the Colours. There is a replica in Salford, together with a cenotaph topped by the sphinx badge. In Bury also is the South African War Memorial, a bronze fusilier in full dress. The Indian Mutiny memorial is in Exeter Cathedral, since the 20th was the East Devonshire Regiment until 1881. It is in the form of a tablet, flanked by two bronze figures in the uniform of 1857.

In 1968, the Regiment merged its separate identity and traditions in the new 'large' regiment, The Royal Regiment of Fusiliers.

Dettingen, Minden, Egmont-op-Zee, Maida, Vimiera, Corunna, Vittoria, Pyrenees, Orthes, Toulouse, Peninsula, Alma, Inkerman, Sevastopol, Lucknow, Khartoum, Relief of Ladysmith, South Africa 1899-1902.

Retreat from Mons, Aisne 1914 '18, Ypres 1915 '17 '18, Somme 1916 '18, Arras 1917 '18, Passchendaele, Cambrai 1917 '18, Hindenburg Line, Macedonia 1915-18, Landing at Helles.

Defence of Escaut, Caen, Medjez el Bab, Sangro, Cassino II, Argenta Gap, Malta 1941-2, Kohima, Chindits 1944, Burma 1943-5.

THE EAST LANCASHIRE REGIMENT

30th Foot raised in 1702 as Sanderson's Marines; 59th Foot in 1741. Linked as 1st and 2nd Bns, The East Lancashire Regt in 1881.

In 1782, the 30th Foot was designated the Cambridgeshire Regiment, and the 59th Foot became the 2nd Nottinghamshire. The new regiment which they formed in 1881 wore white facings, the 1st Battalion march being *The Attack,* and the 2nd's *The Lancashire Lad.*

In the late autumn of 1944, the 1st Battalion was part of the British force which liberated the Dutch city of 's-Hertogenbosch from the Germans. An historian of the campaign, who took part in it himself, wrote: ". . . the honours went to the infantry . . . and above all to the 1st East Lancashires . . . In action almost continuously for five days, often cold and soaked to the skin and with little or no sleep or hot food at a cost of 25 per cent casualties, the will of these men, for the most part children of the Great Depression of the thirties and the drab streets of Lancashire, to close with the enemy never faltered . . ." (*The Battle for Germany,* by H. Essame, published by Batsford).

The museum is in Blackburn Museum, and the Colours are laid up in the Regimental Chapel in Blackburn Cathedral. In 1958 The East Lancashires amalgamated with the South Lancashires to form The Lancashire Regiment. In 1970, a further amalgamation took place with the Loyals to form The Queen's Lancashire Regiment, whose museum is in the Old Sessions House, Preston.

Gibraltar 1704-5, Belleisle, Cape of Good Hope 1806, Corunna, Java, Badajoz, Salamanca, Vittoria, San Sebastian, Nive, Peninsula, Waterloo, Bhurtpore, Alma, Inkerman, Sevastopol, Canton, Ahmed Khel, Afghanistan 1878-80, Chitral, South Africa 1900-02.

Retreat from Mons, Marne 1914, Aisne 1914 '18, Ypres 1914 '17 '18, Neuve Chapelle, Arras 1917 '18, Somme 1916 '18, Helles, Doiran 1917 '18, Kut al Amara 1917.

Dunkirk 1940, Falaise, Lower Maas, Ourthe, Reichswald, Weeze, Aller, Madagascar, Pinwe, Burma 1944-5.

THE SOUTH LANCASHIRE REGIMENT (THE PRINCE OF WALES'S VOLUNTEERS)

40th Foot raised in 1717 as Philip's Regt. 82nd Foot raised in 1793. Linked as 1st and 2nd Bns, The South Lancashire Regt in 1881.

Until 1881, neither of the component regiments had a Lancashire connection. The 40th Foot was the 2nd Somersetshire from 1782, and on its formation, the 82nd was given the title The Prince of Wales's Volunteers, the first commanding officer being a member of the Prince's entourage. This secondary title persisted through the reorganisation of 1881, and the more recent amalgamation with the East Lancashires mentioned above, but has vanished with The Queen's Lancashires of 1970.

The South Lancashires wore buff facings in full dress. The regimental quick march was *God Bless the Prince of Wales* and the slow march was *The Lancashire Witches*.

The old Regimental depot at Peninsula Barracks, Warrington, houses the museum, and the Regimental Chapel containing the Colours and memorials is in the parish church of St. Elphin in Warrington. Among them is a memorial tablet for the South African War, memorial windows for both world wars, and a screen which serves as a memorial for the old 3rd Battalion — the 4th Royal Lancashire Militia. There is a statue in Queen's Gardens, depicting Lt. Col. McCarthy-O'Leary, and in memory of all ranks who fell in the South African War.

Louisburg, Martinique 1762, Havannah, St. Lucia 1778, Monte Video, Rolica, Vimiera, Corunna, Talavara, Badajoz, Salamanca, Vittoria, Pyrenees, Nivelle, Orthes, Toulouse, Peninsula, Niagara, Waterloo, Candahar 1842*, Ghuznee 1842, Cabool 1842*, Maharajpore, Sevastopol, Lucknow, New Zealand, Relief of Ladysmith, South Africa 1899-1902, Afghanistan 1919.

Mons, Aisne 1914 '18, Messines 1914 '17 '18, Ypres 1914 '15 '17 '18, Somme 1916 '18, Lys, Doiran 1917 '18, Sari Bair, Baghdad, Baluchistan 1918.

Dunkirk 1940, Normandy Landing, Bourguebus Ridge, Falaise, Rhineland, North West Europe 1940 '44-5, Madagascar, North Arakan, Kohima, Nyaungu Bridgehead.

* Normally spelled Kandahar and Kabul.

25

THE LOYAL REGIMENT (NORTH LANCASHIRE)

47th Foot raised in 1741 as Mordaunt's Regt. Became the Lancashire Regt in 1782. 81st Regt raised in 1793. Linked as 1st and 2nd Bns in 1881.

At the battle of Quebec in 1759, the 47th were posted in the centre of General Wolfe's line. The General was killed, and in his memory the officers of the 47th thereafter wore a black line in the gold lace of their tunics. In the drab khaki of modern times, this was represented by a black lanyard worn on the left shoulder.

The 'Loyal' element in the title came from the 81st. It was raised at Lincoln, when the militia of that county volunteered 'en masse' to serve as a regular regiment at the start of the war against revolutionary France. In recognition of this patriotic zeal, it was allowed to take the title The Loyal Lincoln Volunteers.

The title of the regiment formed in 1881 was The Loyal North Lancashire. It wore white facings, a cap badge of the royal crest and rose of Lancaster, and as a collar badge, the arms of the city of Lincoln. Its marches were *The Red, Red Rose, The Mountain Rose, The Lincolnshire Poacher,* and as a slow march *The 47th Regiment.*

The museum is in the Old Sessions House, Preston. The Regimental Chapel is in St. John's Church, and the South African War Memorial is in Avenham Park. The world war memorials are in Queen's Park and the parish church, Bolton, and in Corfe Castle church in the Isle of Purbeck. The Loyals, as has already been stated, merged into The Queen's Lancashire Regiment in 1970.

Louisburg, Quebec 1759, Maida, Corunna, Tarifa, Vittoria, San Sebastian, Nive, Peninsula, Ava, Alma, Inkerman, Sevastopol, Ali Masjid, Afghanistan 1878-9, Defence of Kimberley, South Africa 1899-1902.

Mons, Aisne 1914 '18, Ypres 1914 '17 '18, Somme 1916 '18, Lys, Hindenburg Line, Suvla, Gaza, Baghdad, Kilimanjaro.

Dunkirk 1940, Djebel Kesskiss, Gueriat El Aatch Ridge, North Africa 1943, Anzio, Fiesole, Monte Grande, Italy 1944-5, Jahore, Singapore Island.

THE MANCHESTER REGIMENT

*63rd Foot raised in 1757,
96th Foot in 1824. Became
1st and 2nd Bns, The Manchester
Regt in 1881.*

The 63rd was designated the West Suffolk Regiment in 1782. It was the 96th which hailed from Manchester, being actually raised and later quartered there. It inherited its two early battle honours, the sphinx badge for 'Egypt' and 'Peninsula' from a previous 96th Regiment which had been disbanded.

When The Manchester Regiment as such came into being, it wore the arms of the city as its badge, but in 1923 it reverted to the plain fleur-de-lys, which was the badge of the old 63rd. About the same time, it recovered the 63rd's former deep green facings, although opportunities for wearing full dress have proved to be few.

In 1942, the 1st Battalion was in the Singapore garrison, and before the final collapse, a small party of men was sent away to be the nucleus of a reborn battalion in England. They did not succeed in escaping, so to preserve continuity of tradition, the 6th Battalion was renumbered the 1st. 370 of the original battalion died in Japanese camps.

The Manchesters' marches were *The Young May Moon* (63rd's) and *The Manchester* (96th's), with *Farewell Manchester* as the slow step. The regimental collection is in The Old Town Hall, Ashton-under-Lyme, by courtesy of the Tameside Municipality, and the Colours and memorials are in Manchester Cathedral, in the Regimental Chapel. There is a War Memorial at Ardwick Green, Manchester 12.

The Regiment amalgamated with The King's Regiment (Liverpool) in 1958. This was a return to the fold, for the 63rd was originally raised as the 8th Foot's 2nd Battalion.

Guadaloupe 1759, Egmont-op-Zee, Peninsula, Martinique 1809, Guadalope 1810, New Zealand, Alma, Inkerman, Sevastopol, Afghanistan 1879-80, Egypt 1882, Defence of Ladysmith, South Africa 1899-1902.

Mons, Givenchy 1914, Ypres 1915 '17 '18, Somme 1916 '18, Hindenburg Line, Piave, Macedonia 1915-18, Gallipoli 1915, Megiddo, Baghdad.

Dyle, Defence of Arras, Caen, Scheldt, Lower Maas, Roer, Reichswald, Gothic Line, Malta 1940, Kohima.

THE ROYAL LEICESTERSHIRE REGIMENT

17th Foot raised in 1688 as Richard's Regt. Became the Leicestershire Regt in 1782.

This was another regiment whose officers wore a black line in the gold lace of their full dress in memory of General Wolfe. Its band was also accustomed to play a few bars of a lament known as *Wolfe's Lament* when the Regiment was on parade, while all ranks stood to attention.

The royal tiger badge was awarded to the 17th after eighteen years of hard service in India between 1804 and 1823 and the Regiment bore the appropriate nickname of 'The Tigers'. It became a 'Royal' regiment in 1946 and in 1964 the 4th Battalion of the Anglian Regiment. That battalion being disbanded, since 1980 the county designation has been borne by the 2nd.

The Leicestershire wore white facings, changing to pearl grey in 1931. Its march was originally based upon an old Greek air, which came to be thought inappropriate for an English county regiment. In 1933, it was changed to *A Hunting Call*. Leicestershire is fine hunting country, and this old hunting song was in fact the march of the Leicestershire militia. The slow march was *General Monckton 1762*. It was composed in that year in honour of the officer who was then colonel commandant of the 17th Foot.

The museum has been established at The Magazine, Oxford Street, Leicester. The Colours are laid up near by in St. Martin's Church, the Cathedral.

Namur 1695, Louisburg, Martinique 1762, Havannah Hindoostan, Ghuznee 1839, Khelat, Afghanistan 1839, Sevastopol, Ali Masjid, Afghanistan 1878-9, Defence of Ladysmith, South Africa 1889-1902.

Aisne 1914 '18, Neuve Chapelle, Somme 1916 '18, Ypres 1917, Cambrai 1917 '18, Lys, St. Quentin Canal, France & Flanders 1914-18, Palestine 1918, Mesopotamia 1915-18.

Scheldt, North West Europe 1944-5, Sidi Barrani, North Africa 1940-1 '43, Salerno, Gothic Line, Italy 1943-5, Crete, Malaya 1941-2, Chindits 1944, Korea 1951-2.

THE ROYAL LINCOLNSHIRE REGIMENT

10th Foot raised in 1685 as Granville's Regt. Became the North Lincolnshire Regt in 1782

The first Colours carried by the 10th had a yellow ground, and this gave rise to its nickname 'The Yellow Bellies'. Consequently, it wore yellow facings until 1881, when in common with all other English regiments it was compelled by official ukase to change to white. Under normal circumstances, the yellow Regimental Colour would have been exchanged for the St. George's red cross on a white ground carried by all regiments with white facings. By carefully repairing Colours presented in 1863 and 1859, the 1st and 2nd Battalions managed to avoid this for the next century.

The sphinx badge was awarded for service in Egypt in 1801. The 10th came there from India, and endured a 120-mile march across the desert to reach the battle area. Between 1842 and 1858 it was in India again and participated in the Sikh Wars and the Indian Mutiny. As it sailed from Calcutta for home, the Governor General ordered the guns of Fort William to be fired in salute. It became a 'Royal' regiment in 1946.

The Regimental march was *The Lincolnshire Poacher*, and the museum is in the Old Barracks, Burton Road, Lincoln, and St. Mathias' Church there contains several memorials. The Colours are lodged in Lincoln Cathedral. In 1960, the Lincolns amalgamated with the Northamptons to form what is now the 2nd Battalion, The Royal Anglian Regiment. Twenty years later the county designations were restored to the battalion as a supplementary title.

Blenheim, Ramillies, Oudenarde, Malplaquet, Peninsula, Sobraon, Mooltan, Goojerat, Punjaub, Lucknow, Atbara, Khartoum, Paardeberg, South Africa 1900-02.

Mons, Marne 1914, Messines 1914 '17 '18, Ypres 1914 '15 '17, Neuve Chapelle, Loos, Somme 1916 '18, Lys, Hindenburg Line, Suvla.

Dunkirk 1940, Normandy Landing, Fontenoy le Pesnil, Antwerp-Tournhout Canal, North Africa 1943, Salerno, Gothic Line, Ngakyedauk Pass, Burma 1943-5.

THE ROYAL FUSILIERS (CITY OF LONDON REGIMENT)

7th Foot raised in 1685 as the Royal Regt of Fuziliers. Became The City of London Regt in 1881.

One of the two original fusilier regiments, it was raised from the existing garrison of the Tower of London during Monmouth's rebellion. To mark its London links, the Regiment was granted the privilege of marching through the City with drums beating, Colours flying, etc.

Its full dress was the fusilier cap with a white hackle, and blue facings. Its marches were *The British Grenadiers* and *Fighting with the 7th Royal Fusiliers,* which was composed in 1893 as a popular patriotic song.

The museum is in the Tower. 29 Colours, the oldest dated 1793, are in the Regimental Chapel in St. Sepulchre's church, opposite the Old Bailey. Others are in St. Michael's, Cornhill, St. Edmund's in Lombard Street, Kensington Town Hall, Warlingham parish church, and St. Anne's in Manchester. The Crimean Colour is in Winchester Cathedral, the Peninsula Colour in the National Army Museum. Another is at the U.S. Military Academy, West Point, having been captured by the American rebels in 1775.

A large statue at Holborn Bars, opposite the Prudential Insurance Building, forms the Fusiliers' War Memorial, and there are others at Fusilier House in Balham, the Guildhall, and Warlingham, Surrey.

In 1968, the 'large' Royal Regiment of Fusiliers was formed, into which the 7th merged its identity and traditions.

Namur 1695, Martinique 1809, Talavara, Busaco, Albuhera, Badajoz, Salamanca, Vittoria, Pyrenees, Orthes, Toulouse, Peninsula, Alma, Inkerman, Sevastopol, Kandahar 1880, Afghanistan 1879-80, Relief of Ladysmith, South Africa 1899-1902.

Mons, Marne 1914, Ypres 1914 '15 '17 '18, Somme 1916 '18, Arras 1917 '18, Cambrai 1917 '18, Hindenburg Line, Struma, Landing at Helles, Palestine 1918.

Dunkirk 1940, Keren, North Africa 1940 '43, Mozzgrogna, Salerno, Gargiliano Crossing, Anzio, Cassino II, Gothic Line, Cariano, Korea 1952-3.

THE MIDDLESEX REGIMENT (DUKE OF CAMBRIDGE'S OWN)

57th Foot raised in 1755 as 59th; became the West Middlesex Regt in 1782. 77th Foot raised in 1787; became the East Middlesex in 1807. Linked 1881.

The nickname of the Middlesex was 'The Diehards'. At Albuhera in 1811, the 57th lost 428 of its total strength of 647 defending a hill against French attacks. Colonel Inglis, the commanding officer, fell wounded, but lay by the Colours calling out to his men "Die hard, 57th, die hard!"

When the Korean War began in 1950, the 1st Battalion was sent with the Argylls as the first British troops to go to the aid of the hard-pressed Americans. Although the Battalion contained a high proportion of young National Servicemen, it won seven battle honours in the first and most difficult part of the war. Only two could be placed upon the Regimental Colour.

The 77th became 'The Duke of Cambridge's Own' in 1876, he being Commander-in-Chief of the army. The Middlesex facings were yellow. The 1st Battalion's march was *Sir Manley Power,* the 2nd's *Paddy's Resource,* and the slow march *Daughter of the Regiment.* Colours and memorials are in the Regimental Chapel in St. Paul's Cathedral, St. Paul's church (Mill Hill), St Mary's (Hornsey), All Hallow's (Tottenham), St. Leonard's (Shoreditch), St. Nicholas' (Chiswick) and the parish churches of Chipping Barnet and Stoke-on-Trent. There are memorials also in Canterbury Cathedral, and the old depot — Inglis Barracks in Mill Hill. The Museum is at Bruce Castle, Lordship Lane, Tottenham. In 1966 the Regiment was merged into the new 'large' regiment, The Queen's Regiment.

Mysore, Seringapatam, Albuhera, Cuidad Rodrigo, Badajoz, Vittoria, Pyrenees, Nivelle, Nive, Peninsula, Alma, Inkerman, Sevastopol, New Zealand, South Africa 1879, Relief of Ladysmith, South Africa 1900-02.

Mons, Marne 1914, Ypres 1915 '17 '18, Albert 1916 '18, Bazentin, Cambrai 1917 '18, Hindenburg Line, Suvla, Jerusalem, Mesopotamia 1917-18.

Dunkirk 1940, Normandy Landing, Caen, Mont Pincon, Rhine, El Alamein, Akarit, Sicily 1943, Anzio, Hong Kong, Korea 1950-51, Naktong Bridgehead.

THE ROYAL NORFOLK REGIMENT

9th Foot raised in 1685 as Cornwall's Regt. Became the East Norfolk Regt in 1782 and the Norfolk Regt in 1881.

The exact reason for the 9th's adoption of its distinctive Britannia badge is not known for certain. According to tradition, the badge was granted for service at the battle of Almanza in Spain in 1707, in which the regiment suffered heavy casualties. In 1799, it was confirmed as the 9th's privilege.

The Regimental march was, of course, *Rule Britannia,* and the facing colour was yellow. In 1959, the Norfolks and Suffolks amalgamated to form what is now the 1st Battalion, The Royal Anglian Regiment, with the county designation being restored as a supplementary title in 1980.

Five V.C.s were won by Norfolks in the Second World War—more than any other regiment. In the fierce fighting to relieve Kohima in 1944, the 2nd Battalion was in continuous action for seven weeks. Captain John Randle earned one of the V.C.s when he carried out a single-handed charge on a Japanese machine-gun bunker pinning down his men, and dying from several hits, flung himself across the firing slit.

The museum is at Britannia Barracks, Norwich, and the Colours are laid up in the Regimental Chapel in the Cathedral, and in Sandringham church. Other memorials are in Canterbury Cathedral and St. George's Chapel, Windsor.

Belleisle, Havannah, Martinique 1794, Rolica, Vimiera, Corunna, Busaco, Salamanca, Vittoria, San Sebastian, Nive, Peninsula, Cabool 1842, Moodkee, Ferozeshah, Sobraon, Sevastopol, Kabul 1879, Afghanistan 1879-80, Paardeberg, South Africa 1900-02.

Mons, Le Cateau, Marne 1914, Ypres 1914 '15 '17 '18, Somme 1916 '18, Hindenburg Line, Landing at Suvla, Gaza, Shaiba, Kut al Amara 1915 '17.

St. Omer-La Bassee, Normandy Landing, Brieux Bridgehead, Venraij, Rhineland, North West Europe 1940 '44-5, Singapore Island, Kohima, Aradura, Burma 1944-5, Korea 1951-2.

THE NORTHAMPTONSHIRE REGIMENT

48th Foot raised in 1741 as Cholmondeley's Regt. Became the Northamptonshire Regt in 1782. 58th Foot raised in 1755.

The 58th was designated the Rutlandshire Regiment in 1782, at a time when it was part of the garrison of Gibraltar during the great siege. For its services there, it was awarded the castle and key badge. The 58th was also distinguished by being the last British regiment to carry its Colours into action, this during the First Boer War of 1880-1. The Boer marksmen clearly demonstrated that the pageantry of scarlet tunic and standards had no part to play in modern wars, although the former lingered a little longer. The famous Colour is now in the National Army Museum.

The other component of the Northamptonshires' badge, the battle honour 'Talavara', was contributed by the 48th, which had two battalions posted on the ridge which formed the anchor of Wellington's line in the battle of 1809.

The two regiments were linked in 1881, and wore buff facings. The 1st Battalion march was *The Northamptonshire*, and that of the 2nd, *The Lincolnshire Poacher*. The museum is Abington Park Museum, Abington, Northampton, and the Regimental Chapel with the Colours and memorials is in the Church of the Holy Sepulchre, Sheep Street.

In 1960 the Regiment amalgamated with the Lincolnshires to form the 2nd Battalion, The Royal Anglian Regiment, and the county designation was restored as a supplementary title in 1980.

Loiusburg, Quebec 1759, Martinique 1762, Havannah, Martinique 1794, Maida, Duoro, Talavara, Albuhera, Badajoz, Salamanca, Vittoria, Pyrenees, Nivelle, Orthes, Toulouse, Peninsula, New Zealand, Sevastopol, South Africa 1879, Tirah, Modder River, South Africa 1899-1902.

Mons, Marne 1914, Aisne 1914 '18, Ypres 1914 '17, Neuve Chapelle, Loos, Somme 1916 '18, Arras 1917 '18, Epehy, Gaza. North West Europe 1940 '45, North Africa 1942-3, Garigliano Crossing, Anzio, Cassino II, Italy 1943-5, Yu, Imphal, Myinmu Bridgehead, Burma 1943-5.

THE ROYAL NORTHUMBERLAND FUSILIERS

5th Foot raised in 1674 as the 'Irish Regiment' in the Dutch service. Taken into the English army in 1685; became the Northumberland Regt in 1782.

'The Shiners', 'The Old and Bold', 'The Fighting Fifth' ... it became a fusilier regiment in 1836. From its early days it wore facings of a unique colour, gosling green, which it preserved even when it became a 'Royal' regiment in 1935.

In full dress it wore the fusilier cap with a scarlet and white hackle. Its badge was the Garter emblem, St. George and the Dragon, and it kept April 23rd, St. George's Day, with ceremony. Drums and headdress were decked with red and white roses, and a special 'Drummer's Colour' was paraded, a gosling green silk banner which was the property of the officers and allowed to appear officially on this day only.

The marches of the 5th were *The British Grenadiers, Rule Britannia* (in 1778 it served on board ships of the Royal Navy in the West Indies) and, of course, *Blaydon Races*. The museum is in Alnwick Castle, Alnwick and Colours and memorials are in St. Nicholas' Cathedral; and St. Mary's Church, Newcastle, and St. Michael's, Alnwick.

On St. George's Day, 1968, the Regiment merged into The Royal Regiment of Fusiliers, which wears a St. George's badge and a red and white hackle, keeps St. George's Day, and marches to *The British Grenadiers* and *Rule Britannia*. The 1st Battalion has retained the 'Drummer's Colour'.

Wilhelmstahl, St. Lucia 1778, Rolica, Vimiera, Corunna, Busaco, Cuidad Rodrigo, Badajoz, Salamanca, Vittoria, Nivelle, Orthes, Toulouse, Peninsula, Lucknow, Afghanistan 1879-80, Khartoum, Modder River, South Africa 1900-02.

Mons, Marne 1914, Ypres 1914 '15 '17 '18, St. Julien, Somme 1916 '18, Scarpe 1917 '18, Selle, Piave, Struma, Suvla.

Dunkirk 1940, Caen, Rhineland, Sidi Barrani, Defence of Tobruk, Tobruk 1941, Cauldron, El Alamein, Salerno, Cassino II, Imjin, Korea 1950-1.

THE SHERWOOD FORESTERS (NOTTINGHAMSHIRE & DERBYSHIRE REGIMENT)

45th Foot raised in 1741. Became the Nottinghamshire Regt in 1782, and 1st Bn The Sherwood Foresters (The Derbyshire Regt) in 1881.

The battle honours and some of this regiment's history are given under the DERBYSHIRE entry.

The 45th gained its nickname 'The Old Stubborns' in the hard fighting of the Peninsular War. The fiercest action was the siege of Badajoz in 1812. The main British assaults on the walls were made after a 12-day artillery bombardment, and were all beaten off. In the end, a volunteer storming party did manage to penetrate the fortress in spite of heavy casualties. A subaltern of the 45th tore down the French flag, and having no British flag to hand, hoisted his scarlet coatee to signify success. In commemoration, the Foresters hoisted a red jacket to their flagstaff on the anniversary of the event.

In 1866 the 45th adopted the title 'Sherwood Foresters' which originated with the Nottinghamshire Militia who were granted the title 'The Royal Sherwood Foresters' in 1814. The full county designation, lost in 1881, was restored in 1902 and the former Lincoln green facings in 1913. It is of interest that one of the Territorial battalions, the 7th, were The Robin Hood Rifles and, since the regimental badge is illustrated elsewhere, this battalion's badge is shown above.

The Regimental marches were *The Young May Moon* and *I'm Ninety-Five,* the first being an Irish tune used in the comic-opera *Robin Hood,* and the latter the march of the original 95th Foot, The Rifle Brigade. An unofficial march was *The Derby Ram,* an eighteenth century Jacobite song. The museum is in Nottingham Castle, which also contains many of the Colours, and there are collections in the Derby Museum and Art Gallery, The Strand, Derby, and the Newark Musem, Appletongate, Newark, Nottinghamshire.

In 1970, The Foresters amalgamated with The Worcestershire Regiment to form The Worcestershire and Sherwood Foresters Regiment.

THE OXFORDSHIRE & BUCKINGHAMSHIRE LIGHT INFANTRY

43rd Foot raised in 1741; 52nd Foot in 1755. Latter became the Oxfordshire Regt in 1782. Linked as 1st and 2nd Bns in 1881.

The 43rd and 52nd first fought together at the battle of Bunker Hill in 1775, were selected for Sir John Moore's experimental training camp in 1803 and became the original Light Infantry regiments the same year. The 43rd was the Monmouthshire regiment until 1881.

In the Second World War, the 52nd served as glider-borne troops, and provided the first formations to land in Europe on D-Day. Their task was to seize bridges beyond the landing beaches by surprise glider descents, hence the unique battle honour 'Pegasus Bridge', from the Airborne troops' Pegasus badge.

The Regiment wore white facings. Its marches were *Lower Castle Yard* (52nd's), *Nachtlager en Grenada* (43rd's), and *The Italian Song,* a soldiers' song picked up by the 4th (Territorial) Battalion when serving in Italy in 1918.

There are two museums: one at Slade Park, Headington, where there is also a Boer War memorial statue, and the other with The Royal Green Jackets at Winchester. The latter contains the diamond star presented to Moore by the 52nd's officers, when he received the Order of the Bath. The Colours are laid up in Christchurch, Oxford. In 1966, the Regiment became the 1st Battalion, Royal Green Jackets.

Quebec 1759, Martinique 1762, Havannah, Mysore, Hindoostan, Martinique 1794, Vimiera, Corunna, Busaco, Fuentes d'Onor, Cuidad Rodrigo, Badajoz, Salamanca, Vittoria, Pyrenees, Nivelle, Nive, Orthes, Toulouse, Peninsula, Waterloo, South Africa 1851'2'3, Delhi 1857, New Zealand, Relief of Kimberley, Paardeberg, South Africa 1900-02.
Mons, Ypres 1914 '17, Langemarck 1914 '17, Nonne Bosschen, Somme 1916 '18, Cambrai 1917 '18, Piave, Doiran 1917 '18, Ctesiphon, Defence of Kut al Amara.
Cassel, Ypres-Commines Canal, Normandy Landing, Pegasus Bridge, Reichswald, Rhine, Enfidaville, Salerno, Anzio, Gemmano Ridge.

THE KING'S SHROPSHIRE LIGHT INFANTRY

53rd Foot raised in 1755, becoming the Shropshire Regt in 1782. For details of 85th Foot, see the BUCKINGHAMSHIRE *entry. Linked as 1st and 2nd Bns in 1881.*

The 53rd had red facings, and was in consequence nicknamed 'The Brickdusts'. The 85th was 'The Young Bucks', to distinguish it from the other, and more senior Buckinghamshire regiment, the 16th Foot, 'The Old Bucks'.

The 85th was converted to light infantry in 1808, and as such campaigned in the Peninsula and the U.S.A., being part of the force which burned Washington in 1814. It achieved such a fine reputation that it was designated The Duke of York's Own, that worthy being Commander-in-Chief of the army. In 1821, the 85th became The King's.

The two regiments were linked in 1881, the 53rd being transformed into light infantry and losing its red facings but retaining its Shropshire connection, the 85th preserving its royal title and blue facings, but moving its depot from Oxford to Shrewsbury.

The K.S.L.I. marches were *Farmer's Boy, Old Towler* and *Daughter of the Regiment.* Its museum is in The Castle, Shrewsbury, and contains some of the Colours. Others, with the Regiment's memorials, are in its Chapel at The Quarry, Shrewsbury, and in St. Mary's Church, Shrewsbury.

In 1968 the Regiment became the 3rd Battalion of the new 'large regiment', The Light Infantry.

Nieuport, Tournay, St. Lucia 1796, Talavara, Fuentes d'Onor, Salamanca, Vittoria, Pyrenees, Nivelle, Nive, Toulouse, Peninsula, Bladensburg, Aliwal, Sobraon, Goojerat, Punjaub, Lucknow, Afghanistan 1879-80, Egypt 1882, Suakin 1885, Paardeberg, South Africa 1899-1902.
Armentieres 1914, Ypres 1915 '17, Frezenberg, Somme 1916 '18, Arras 1917 '18, Cambrai 1917 '18, Bligny, Epehy, Doiran 1917 '18, Jerusalem.
Dunkirk 1940, Normandy Landing, Antwerp, Venraij, Hochwald, Bremen, North West Europe 1940, 44-5, Tunis, Anzio, Italy 1943-5, Kowang-San, Korea 1951-2.

THE SOMERSET LIGHT INFANTRY (PRINCE ALBERT'S)

13th Foot raised in 1685 as the Earl of Huntingdon's Regt. Became the 1st Somersetshire Regt in 1782.

The 13th became light infantry in 1822, and was part of the 1838 expedition which marched into Afghanistan to support a friendly ruler. Later, the British force was massacred as it withdrew from Kabul. Of 17,000 soldiers and camp-followers, only one survivor, Dr. Brydon, got through to the 13th garrisoning Jellalabad. The Afghans besieged Jellalabad for three months, and when the relief force arrived, the 13th's band played it in with the air *Oh! but ye've been lang o'coming!* For its gallant defence of the town, the 13th was awarded the mural crown badge, the title Prince Albert's Own, and the right to blue facings although a 'non-royal' regiment.

Sergeants of the 13th wore their sashes over the left shoulder, instead of the normal right. This perhaps commemorated the battle of Culloden in 1746 when, with most of the officers casualties, the sergeants took charge.

The Regiment's march was *Prince Albert*. Its museum is in The Castle, Taunton, and holds the Colours. Memorials and Colours of Territorial and Service Battalions are in St. Mary's church, Taunton, Bath Abbey, the Minster at Ilminster, and Burrington church. The dead of the Afghan War have their memorial in Canterbury Cathedral.

Amalgamated with the Duke of Cornwall's Light Infantry in 1959, the Somersets formed the 1st Battalion, The Light Infantry in 1968.

Gibraltar 1704-5, Dettingen, Martinique 1809, Ava, Ghuznee 1839, Afghanistan 1839, Cabool 1842*, Sevastopol, South Africa 1878-9, Burma 1885-7, Relief of Ladysmith, South Africa 1899-1902, Afghanistan 1919.

Marne 1914 '18, Aisne 1914, Ypres 1915 '17 '18, Somme 1916 '18, Albert 1916 '18, Arras 1917 '18, Cambrai 1917 '18, Hindenburg Line, Palestine 1917-18, Tigris 1916.

Hill 112, Mont Pincon, Rhineland, Rhine, North West Europe 1944-5, Cassino II, Corina Canal Crossing, Italy 1944-5, North Arakan, Ngakyedauk Pass.

* This is more frequently spelled **Kabul.**

THE SOUTH STAFFORDSHIRE REGIMENT

38th Foot raised in 1705 as Lillingstone's Regt. Became 1st Staffordshire Regt in 1782. 80th or Staffordshire Volunteers raised in 1793.

The 38th spent a record number of its early years — 1707 to 1764 — in the unhealthiest station the British army then possessed, the West Indies. During that time it developed probably the first form of tropical dress, making up breeches and waistcoats from light sacking or 'ticking' used locally for bagging sugar. This is the origin of the commemorative buff holland patch worn by the Regiment behind its cap badges.

The badge itself is the ancient badge of the Stafford family, the Stafford knot, worn by both the 38th and the 80th from the late eighteenth century. The 80th was raised from volunteers from the Staffordshire Militia and the two were linked as 1st and 2nd Battalions, The South Staffordshire Regiment in 1881. Its facings were yellow, and its marches *Come Lasses and Lads* and *The 80th.*

Other distinctives gained by the Regiment were the Sphinx, superscribed 'Egypt', borne on the Colours and the glider badge worn on the uniform sleeves, an honour shared with the Border Regiment. The Colours are lodged in Lichfield Cathedral and the museum is at Whittington Barracks, Lichfield. In 1959 the South and North Staffordshires amalgamated.

Guadaloupe 1759, Martinique 1762, Monte Video, Rolica, Vimiero, Corunna, Busaco, Badajoz, Salamanca, Vittoria, St Sebastian, Nive, Peninsula, Ava, Moodkee, Ferozeshah, Sobraon, Pegu, Alma, Inkerman, Sevastopol, Lucknow, Central India, South Africa 1878-9, Egypt 1882, Kirbekan, Nile 1884-5, South Africa 1900-02.

Mons, Marne 1914, Aisne 1914 '18, Ypres 1914 '17, Loos, Somme 1916 '18, Cambrai 1917 '18, St. Quentin Canal, Vittorio Veneto, Suvla.

Caen, Noyers, Falaise, Arnhem 1944, North West Europe 1940 '44, North Africa 1940, Landing in Sicily, Sicily 1943, Chindits 1944, Burma 1944.

THE NORTH STAFFORDSHIRE REGIMENT (THE PRINCE OF WALES'S)

64th Foot raised in 1756. Became the 2nd Staffordshire Regt in 1782. 98th Foot raised in 1824.

As with the other Staffordshire regiment, the 64th spent most of its early life on the other side of the Atlantic Ocean. From 1759 to 1803, its foreign service was performed in West Indies or America, and afterwards it saw action in India and China, for which latter service it was awarded the Dragon superscribed 'China' to be borne on its colours.

The 98th had no county affiliation, but in 1876 was given the title The Prince of Wales's. The two regiments were linked in 1881 as the 1st and 2nd Battalions, The North Staffordshire Regiment. It wore black facings, and a badge composed of both the Stafford knot and the Prince of Wales's plume.

The Regimental quick march was *The Days we went a-gypsying,* and its slow march the appropriate *God Bless the Prince of Wales.* Its museum is the same as for the South Staffordshires, and its memorials and Colours are to be likewise found in the barracks and Lichfield Cathedral. Territorial Battalion Colours and memorials are in the parish churches of Stoke-on-Trent and Burton-on-Trent.

As already stated, the North Staffordshires have merged into The Staffordshire Regiment. The new regiment's badge includes the Stafford knot, the crown and the Prince of Wales's plume. The South Staffordshire badge backing is also retained.

Guadaloupe 1759, Martinique 1794, St. Lucia 1803, Surinam, Punjaub, Reshire, Bushire, Koosh-ab, Persia, Lucknow, Hafir, South Africa 1900-02, Afghanistan 1919.

Armentieres 1914, Somme 1916 '18, Arras 1917, Messines 1917 '18, Ypres 1917 '18, St. Quentin Canal, Selle, Sari Bair, Kut al Amara 1917, North West Frontier India 1915.

Dyle, Ypres-Commines Canal, Caen, Brieux Bridgehead, Medjez Plain, North Africa 1943, Anzio, Rome, Marradi, Burma 1943.

THE SUFFOLK REGIMENT

12th Foot raised in 1685 as the Duke of Norfolk's Regt. Became the East Suffolk Regt in 1782.

This was one of the six Minden regiments (see page 17) and its badge bore the castle and key for its part in the defence of Gibraltar, 1779-83. One of the great episodes in the Regiment's history, however, had nothing to do with war. In 1852, a draft of 55 men for the 12th, with an officer, was on board H.M.S. *Birkenhead*. Altogether, there were some 360 young soldiers on the ship, as well as soldiers' families, bound for South Africa. In the middle of the night, she struck a rock and foundered. Only three boats could be launched, and the men stood fast while the women and children entered them. Few of the soldiers could swim, but none broke the ranks to rush for a last chance of life in the overcrowded boats. There were very few survivors, and in St. Mary's church in Bury St. Edmunds there is a memorial tablet to the 12th's *Birkenhead* heroes.

The Suffolks wore yellow facings in full dress, and their quick march was *Speed the Plough*. The Museum is in The Keep at Gibraltar Barracks, Bury St. Edmunds — the old depot — and the Colours are laid up in the Regimental Chapel in St. Mary's church.

In 1959, the Regiment amalgamated with the Royal Norfolk Regiment to form the 1st East Anglian Regiment. In 1964, this became the 1st Battalion, the Royal Anglian Regiment and in 1980 the county connection was restored by adding its name as a supplementary battalion title.

Dettingen, Minden, Seringapatam, India, South Africa 1851-2-3, New Zealand, Afghanistan 1878-80, South Africa 1900-02.

Le Cateau, Neuve Chapelle, Ypres 1915 '17 '18, Somme 1916 '18, Arras 1917 '18, Cambrai 1917 '18, Hindenburg Line, Macedonia 1915-18, Landing at Suvla, Gaza.

Dunkirk 1940, Normandy Landing, Odon, Falaise, Venraij, Brinkum, Singapore Island, North Arakan, Imphal, Burma 1943-5.

THE QUEEN'S ROYAL REGIMENT (WEST SURREY)

2nd Foot raised in 1661 as the Tangier Regt became the Royal West Surrey Regt in 1881.

This was one of the foundation regiments of the English army, raised to garrison Tangiers. On October 10th, 1961, a monument bearing the Regiment's Paschal Lamb badge was unveiled on Putney Heath to mark the exact spot where the Tangiers Regiment first mustered, 1,000 strong, exactly three hundred years before.

It became The Queen's Regiment in 1727, and carried two other badges on the Regimental Colour—the sphinx for service in Egypt, and the naval crown. The latter was awarded in 1909 to commemorate the presence of detachments of The Queen's on board ships of the Royal Navy as marines at the battle of The Glorious First of June in 1794. The Regiment also possessed an unofficial third Colour in its old green facing colour, which had been carefully preserved from the early eighteenth century. Despite an official ban on its use by no less a person than King William IV, it was paraded on certain ceremonial occasions.

As Tangiers was the royal dowry of Charles II's consort, Catherine of Braganza, the Regiment's march was *Braganza*. It wore royal blue facings. The museum is in Clandon Park, West Clandon, Guildford. The Colours and memorials are in Holy Trinity church, Guildford and in Guildford Cathedral. In 1959 The Queen's amalgamated with the East Surreys.

Tangiers 1662-80, Namur 1695, Vimiera, Corunna, Salamanca, Vittoria, Pyrenees, Nivelle, Toulouse, Peninsula, Ghuznee 1839, Khelat, Afghanistan 1839, South Africa 1851-2-3, Taku Forts, Pekin 1860, Burma 1885-7, Tirah, Relief of Ladysmith, South Africa 1899-1902, Afghanistan 1919.

Retreat from Mons, Ypres 1914 '17 '18, Somme 1916 '18, Messines 1917, Vittorio Veneto, Macedonia 1916-17, Gallipoli 1915, Palestine 1917-18, Mesopotamia 1915-18, North West Frontier India 1916-17.

Villiers Bocage, Tobruk 1941, El Alamein, Medenine, Salerno, Monte Gamino, Anzio, Gemmano Ridge, North Arakan, Kohima.

THE EAST SURREY REGIMENT

31st Foot raised in 1702 as Villiers' Marines. 70th Foot raised in 1756, becoming the Surrey Regt in 1782.

From 1782 until it was linked with the 70th as the 1st and 2nd Battalions, The East Surreys, the 31st Foot was officially the Huntingdonshire Regiment. The 70th had begun life as the 31st's 2nd Battalion, so the 1881 arrangement was a family reunion!

The early service of the 31st as marines was recalled in the quick step of the Regiment's 1st Battalion, *A Southerly Wind and a Cloudy Sky,* and the other Regimental march *A Life on the Ocean Wave.* The slow march was *Lord Charles Montague's Huntingdonshire March,* another obvious reference to past connections. The 2nd Battalion's quick march was *The Lass o'Gowrie,* for the 70th had been briefly designated the Glasgow Lowland Regiment between 1813 and 1825.

The East Surrey facings were white and its badge was based upon the arms of Guildford. When it amalgamated with The Queen's to form The Queen's Royal Surrey Regiment, the crown and star formed part of the new badge, and can be seen on the Putney Heath memorial mentioned on page 42.

The museum is housed with The Queen's, but the East Surrey Chapel and the Colours are in All Saints church, Kingston-on-Thames. There are other Colours and memorials in Canterbury Cathedral and St. Mary's church, Huntingdon. In 1966 the new Surrey regiment became the 1st Battalion, The Queen's Regiment.

Gibraltar 1704-5, Dettingen, Martinique 1794, Talavara, Guadaloupe 1810, Albuhera, Vittoria, Pyrenees, Nivelle, Nive, Orthes, Peninsula, Cabool 1842, Moodkee, Ferozeshah, Aliwal, Sobraon, Sevastopol, Taku Forts, New Zealand, Afghanistan 1878-9, Suakin 1885, Relief of Ladysmith, South Africa 1899-1902.

Mons, Marne 1914, La Bassee 1914, Ypres 1915 '17 '18, Loos, Somme 1916 '18, Albert 1916 '18, Cambrai 1917 '18, Selle, Doiran 1918.

Dunkirk 1940, North West Europe 1940, Oued Zarga, Longstop Hill 1943, North Africa 1942-3, Sicily 1943, Sangro, Cassino, Italy 1943-5, Malaya 1941-2.

THE ROYAL SUSSEX REGIMENT

35th Foot raised in 1701 as the Earl of Donegall's Regt. Became the Sussex Regt in 1804.

In 1782 the 35th was designated the Dorsetshire Regiment. Charles Lennox, fourth Duke of Richmond, became its colonel, filled it with Sussex recruits, and persuaded the authorities to transfer the county title to it from the 25th Foot. It was this Duke who gave the ball in Brussels on the eve of the battle of Waterloo. The 35th became a 'Royal' regiment in 1832.

In 1881 it was linked as 1st and 2nd Battalions to the 107th Bengal Infantry, which had been raised in 1854 by the East India Company as its 3rd Bengal European Regiment and had been taken into the British army in 1861.

The Regiment wore blue facings and a badge which featured the Roussillon plume, gained by beating the French Royal Roussillon Regiment at Quebec. The 1st Battalion quick march was *Royal Sussex*, the 2nd's *The Lass of Richmond Hill*. The slow march was *Roussillon*. A popular march within the Regiment was *Sussex by the Sea*, written in 1907.

The museum is in the Redoubt, Eastbourne, and the Regimental Chapel in Chichester Cathedral. Colours are laid up there and in the parish churches at Hastings and Horsham. There are memorials opposite the west pier and the Royal Pavilion, Brighton, and opposite the pier at Eastbourne. The Regiment has merged into the 3rd Battalion, The Queen's Regiment. The battalion collar badge includes the Roussillion plume.

Gibraltar 1704-5, Louisburg, Quebec 1759, Martinique 1762, Havannah, St. Lucia 1778, Maida, Egypt 1882, Abu Klea, Nile 1884-5, South Africa 1900-02, Afghanistan 1919.

Retreat from Mons, Marne 1914 '18, Ypres 1914 '17 '18, Somme 1916 '18, Pilckem, Hindenburg Line, Italy 1917-18, Gallipoli 1915, Palestine 1917-18, North West Frontier India 1915 '16-17.

North West Europe 1940, Abyssinia 1941, Omars, Alam el Halfa, El Alamein, Akarit, North Africa 1940-3, Cassino II, Italy 1944-5, Burma 1943-5.

THE ROYAL WARWICKSHIRE FUSILIERS

6th Foot raised in 1674 for the Dutch service. Taken into the English army in 1688. Became 1st Warwickshire Regt in 1782.

The 6th became a 'Royal' regiment in 1832 and wore blue facings in full dress, but never wore the fusilier cap as it was not designated a fusilier regiment until 1963, when it was put into the transient Fusilier Brigade. Subsequently it merged its traditions into the 'large' regiment, The Royal Regiment of Fusiliers.

The antelope was the long-established badge of the 6th Foot, and was said to have originated from the standard of a Spanish regiment which it captured at Saragossa in 1710. In later times the Warwickshires kept an antelope mascot, a tradition maintained in the new regiment.

The marches of the Regiment were *The Warwickshire Lads*, *McBean's March* and *The Saucy Sixth*. The museum is in St. John's House in Warwick, and the Colours are laid up in St. Mary's church. There is one stand of Territorial Battalion Colours in Coventry Cathedral.

The 2nd Warwickshire Regiment was the 24th Foot, raised in 1689. A second battalion for it was in fact raised in Warwick in 1804, and gained a magnificent fighting record in Spain. Both battalions of the 24th were involved in the Zulu War, the 1st in the tragedy of Isandhlwana, the 2nd in the gallant defence of Rorke's Drift in 1879. It was at the time a Warwickshire Regiment, contained Warwickshiremen, and St. Mary's housed its memorial and Colours. In 1881 it became The South Wales Borderers.

Namur 1695, Martinique 1794, Rolica, Vimiero, Corunna, Vittoria, Pyrenees, Nivelle, Orthes, Peninsula, Niagara, South Africa 1846-7, 1851-2-3, Atbara, Khartoum, South Africa 1899-1902.

Le Cateau, Ypres 1914-15-17, Marne 1914, Somme 1914-15, Arras 1917-18, Lys, Hindenburg Line, Piave, Sari Bair, Baghdad.

Defence of Escaut, Wormhoudt, Ypres-Commines Canal, Normandy Landing, Caen, Mont Pincon, Venrail, Bremen, North West Europe 1940, 44-45, Burma 1945.

THE WILTSHIRE REGIMENT (DUKE OF EDINBURGH'S)

62nd Foot raised in 1756. Became the Wiltshire Regt in 1782. 99th or Lanarkshire Regt raised in 1824. Linked as 1st and 2nd Bns in 1881.

The 62nd were heavily involved in the campaigning of the American rebellion. They acted as light infantry, and acquired their nickname 'The Springers'—"Spring up!" being the light infantry command for "Advance!" When the British army was forced to surrender at Saratoga, the officers of the 62nd tore the Colours from their pikes to prevent them falling into rebel hands, and one of these, after much wandering, was restored to the Regiment in 1927.

During the First Sikh War, the 62nd participated in the two-day battle of Ferozeshah. Set to advance in the open and without support against the strongest part of the Sikh defences, they kept it up for twenty minutes against point-blank artillery fire. They lost over half their number, most of the officers fell and the Colours were brought out of action by the sergeants. On the anniversary of the battle thereafter, the Colours were handed over to the Sergeants' Mess for safe keeping.

The 99th was raised in Glasgow, and became The Duke of Edinburgh's in 1874 in time to add the ducal coronet and cypher to the badge of the Wiltshires.

The Regiment wore unique facings of salmon buff, and marched to *The Wiltshires*, a county song with the refrain *The Vly be on the Turmat*. The museum is in The Wardrobe, 58 The Close, Salisbury, and the Colours are laid up in St. James's church in Devizes and in Salisbury Cathedral. The first Colours of the 99th are lodged in St. Giles's Church, Edinburgh. In 1959, the Wiltshires were amalgamated with the Royal Berkshires.

Louisburg, Nive, Peninsula, New Zealand, Ferozeshah, Sobraon, Sevastopol, Pekin 1860, South Africa 1879, 1900-02.

Mons, Messines 1914 '17, Ypres 1914 '17, Somme 1916 '18, Arras 1917, Bapaume 1918, Macedonia 1915-18, Gallipoli 1915-16, Palestine 1917-18, Baghdad.

Defence of Arras, Hill 112, Maltot, Mont Pincon, Seine 1944, Cleve, Gargliano Crossing, Anzio, Rome, North Arakan.

THE WORCESTERSHIRE REGIMENT

29th Foot raised in 1694 as Farrington's Regt. Became the Worcestershire Regt in 1782. 36th Foot raised in 1701 as Charlemont's Regt.

Colonel Thomas Farrington who raised the 29th was a member of the Coldstream Guards, as were several of the later commanding officers. This accounts for the similarity of the star badge of the 29th and the Coldstream. A larger version used to be worn on the black ammunition wallets, and when the old cross-belt equipment was discontinued a century ago, the Worcestershires received special permission to wear their stars on their issue packs, even into drab khaki days.

The 29th were nicknamed 'The Ever-Sworded'. In 1746, an unprepared detachment was massacred in North America, and to prevent another surprise, the officers wore their swords off duty in their Mess afterwards.

The motto *Firm* borne on the badge and the Colours belonged to the 36th, the Herefordshire Regiment, which became the 2nd Battalion of the Worcestershires in 1881. Another badge carried on the Colour was the naval crown awarded for service as marines at the battle of the Glorious First of June in 1794. For this reason, one of the marches of the Regiment was *Hearts of Oak*. The quick march was *Royal Windsor* and the slow march *Duchess of Kent*. The full dress facings were grass green. The museum is in the City Museum, Foregate Street, Worcester, and the Colours are laid up in Worcester Cathedral and Norton church, with memorials in the former and in Pershore Abbey. In 1970 the Regiment amalgamated with The Sherwood Foresters.

Ramillies, Belleisle, Mysore, Hindoostan, Rolica, Vimiera, Corunna, Talavara, Albuhera, Salamanca, Pyrenees, Nivelle, Nive, Orthes, Toulouse, Peninsula, Ferozeshah, Sobraon, Chillianwallah, Goojerat, Punjaub, South Africa 1900-02.
Mons, Ypres 1914 '15 '17 '18, Gheluvelt, Neuve Chapelle, Somme 1916-18, Cambrai 1917 '18, Lys, Italy 1917-18, Gallipoli 1915-16, Baghdad.
Mont Pincon, Seine 1944, Geilenkirchen, Goch, North West Europe 1940, '44-5, Keren, Gazala, Kohima, Mandalay, Burma 1944-5.

THE WEST YORKSHIRE REGIMENT (THE PRINCE OF WALES'S OWN)

14th Foot raised in 1685 as Hales's Regt. Became the West Yorkshire Regt in 1881.

As already explained under BUCKINGHAMSHIRE, the West Yorkshires eventually arrived at York by way of Bedfordshire and Buckinghamshire. It was chiefly from the latter county that a third battalion for the 14th was raised in 1813. It had seen no active service and was awaiting disbandment in England when Napoleon escaped from Elba. The disbandment order was cancelled and the raw battalion—mostly youths under 20 years of age—was rushed across the Channel to win the battle honour 'Waterloo' for the regiment.

The 1st Battalion was then in India, performing the 23 years of continuous service in that part of the world which gained it the royal tiger badge in 1831. In 1873 it was awarded another Colour badge, the white horse of Hanover, formerly worn by the grenadiers. Finally, when the Prince of Wales presented new Colours to the 1st Battalion in India in 1876, it received both his title and his plume as a Colour badge.

The West Yorkshires wore buff facings, and marched to the French revolutionaries' tune *Ca Ira,* 'borrowed' from the enemy in a battle in 1793. The museum is in the Yorkshire Regiment's Museum, Tower Street, York, and the Colours and memorials are in the Regimental Chapel in York Minster. Colours are also lodged in Bradford Cathedral and the parish churches of Leeds and Halifax. In 1958 the Regiment amalgamated with the East Yorkshires to form the Prince of Wales' Own Regiment of Yorkshire.

Namur 1695, Tournay, Corunna, Java, Waterloo, Bhurtpore, Sevastopol, New Zealand, Afghanistan 1879-80, Relief of Ladysmith, South Africa 1899-1902.

Armentieres 1914, Neuve Chapelle, Somme 1916 '18, Ypres 1917 '18, Cambrai 1917 '18, Villers Bretonneux, Lys, Tardenois, Piave, Suvla.

Keren, Defence of Alamein Line, Pegu 1942, Yenangyaung 1942, Maungdaw, Defence of Sinzweya, Imphal, Bishenpur, Meiktila, Sittang 1945.

THE EAST YORKSHIRE REGIMENT (THE DUKE OF YORK'S OWN)
15th Foot raised in 1685 as Clifton's Regt. Became the York, East Riding, Regt in 1782.

The 15th fought under General Wolfe at Louisburg and Quebec, and the anniversary of the latter battle was celebrated as a regimental day with appropriate ceremonial and festivity. The officers also wore the black line in the gold lace of their full dress tunics in his memory. Bunches of white roses (for Yorkshire) were carried on the pikes of the Colours on Quebec Day, and also on any other parade at which royalty were present. It was the custom in the Regiment for a young officer detailed to carry a Colour for the first time to invite the Colour Party and Escort to drink a glass of champagne with him after the parade.

The Regiment's nickname was 'The Snappers', which originated during the American rebellion. The 15th ran out of ammunition while in action and snapped the locks on their empty muskets to put up an appearance of firing to confuse the enemy.

The full dress facings were white, and the quick march was *The Yorkshire Lass*, with *The 15th von England* as the slow march. The museum is at 11 Butcher Row, Beverley, and there is also material at the Yorkshire Regiment's Museum, York. The Regimental Chapel containing most of the Colours and memorials is in Beverley Minster and others are in Holy Trinity church, Hull. There are war memorials in Londesborough Barracks in Hull, and in Fulford village a cottage home was erected by the father of an officer of the Regiment killed in the Boer War, in memory of his son and other ranks who fell.

In 1958 the Regiment amalgamated with the West Yorkshires.

Blenheim, Ramillies, Oudenarde, Malplaquet, Louisburg, Quebec 1759, Martinique 1762, Havannah, St. Lucia 1778, Martinique 1794, 1809, Guadaloupe 1810, Afghanistan 1879-80, South Africa 1900-02.
Aisne 1914 '18, Armentieres 1914, Ypres 1915 '17 '18, Loos, Somme 1916 '18, Arras 1917 '18, Cambrai 1917 '18, Selle, Doira 1940, Gallipoli 1915.
Dunkirk 1940, Normandy Landing, Odon, Schaddenhof, North West Europe 1940 '44-5, Gazala, El Alamein, Mareth, Sicily 1943, Burma 1942-5.

THE GREEN HOWARDS (ALEXANDRA, PRINCESS OF WALES'S OWN YORKSHIRE REGIMENT)

19th Foot raised in 1688 as Lutterell's Regiment. Became the 1st Yorkshire, North Riding, Regt in 1782.

The 19th was originally raised in the Exeter area, and by chance so was the 2nd Battalion which existed between 1858 and 1956. However, in 1873 the regimental depot was established in Richmond, and Yorkshire has been the Regiment's home ever since. The museum is in Trinity Church Square, Richmond, and the Regimental Chapel with the Colours is in St. Mary's church. Colours of the Service Battalions of the First World War are in County Hall, Northallerton. The museum contains one of the muskets with which the regiment was issued on its formation, together with a rare cartridge bandolier — twelve wooden bottles holding the powder charge, and known to contemporary soldiers as 'The Twelve Apostles'.

The Regiment's official title began as a nickname, appearing in the 1740s when there were two regiments commanded by a Howard, the 3rd, which wore buff facings, and the 19th which wore green. It took a twenty-year verbal battle with the War Office for the 19th to recover its green facings after the 1881 change to white. Even more surprisingly, the authorities agreed to accept the unusual title The Green Howards in 1920.

The 19th became Princess Alexandra's in 1875, when she presented new Colours to the 1st Battalion. She was of the Danish royal family, and the Regiment's badge is the initial letter of her name entwined with the Dannebrog or Danish Cross. Its march is *The Bonnie English Rose*.

Malplaquet, Alma, Inkerman, Sevastopol, Tirah, Relief of Kimberley, Paardeberg, South Africa 1899-1902.

Ypres 1914 '15 '17, Loos, Somme 1916 '18, Arras 1917 '18, Messines 1917 '18, Valenciennes, Sambre, France & Flanders 1914-18, Vittorio Veneto, Suvla.

Norway 1940, Normandy Landing, North West Europe 1940 '44-5, Gazala, El Alemein, Mareth, Akarit, Sicily 1953, Minturno, Anzio.

50

THE DUKE OF WELLINGTON'S REGIMENT (WEST RIDING)

33rd Foot raised in 1702 as Huntingdon's Regt. Became the 1st Yorkshire, West Riding, Regt in 1782. 76th Foot raised in 1787. Linked as 1st and 2nd Bns in 1881.

Arthur Wellesley, the first Duke of Wellington, was a subaltern in the 76th in 1787, and a major in the 33rd in 1793. In those days, officers purchased their commissions, moving as quickly from regiment to regiment as opportunity and private wealth allowed. Wellesley himself became a Lieutenant-Colonel in six years, and later declared that he preferred the Order of The Garter as a decoration because there was 'no damned nonsense about merit' attached to it. He was colonel of the 33rd from 1806 to 1816, during which time he became the victor of the Peninsula and Waterloo, and a field marshal. In 1853, the year after his death, Queen Victoria granted the 33rd a secondary title—The Duke of Wellington's —in his honour. It was an unusually thoughtful act on the part of officialdom to link the 76th with it in 1881. It assumed the present title in 1920 and is the only British regiment to be named after a non-royal personage. His crest is the Regiment's badge.

The Regiment had the only scarlet facings in the army. Its marches are *On Ilkley Moor B'at T'at, I'm Ninety-Five, Scotland the Brave* and *The Wellesley*. Its museum is in the Bankfield Museum, Akroyd Park, Halifax (and contains the Duke's camp bed) and the Colours and memorials are in York Minster and Halifax parish church.

Dettingen, Mysore, Seringapatam, Ally Ghur, Delhi 1803, Leswarree, Deig, Corunna, Nive, Peninsula, Waterloo, Alma, Inkerman, Sevastopol, Abyssinia, Relief of Kimberley, Paardeberg, South Africa 1900-02, Afghanistan 1919.
Mons, Marne 1914 '18, Ypres 1914 '15 '17, Hill 60, Somme 1916 '18, Arras 1917 '18, Cambrai 1917 '18, Lys, Piave, Landing at Suvla.
Dunkirk, St. Valery-en-Caux, Fontenoy le Pesnil, North West Europe 1940 '44-5, Djebel bou Aoukaz 1943, Anzio, Monte Ceco, Sittang 1942, Chindits 1944, Burma 1942-4, The Hook 1953, Korea 1952-3.

THE KING'S OWN YORKSHIRE LIGHT INFANTRY

51st Foot raised in 1755. Became 2nd Yorkshire, West Riding, Regt in 1782.

The originator of the light infantry, Sir John Moore, received his first commission in the 51st. He was killed at the battle of Corunna in 1809, which is one of the Regiment's battle honours. The 51st became a light infantry corps the same year, and was designated The King's Own in 1821.

The K.O.Y.L.I. badge is described as 'a French horn, with a white rose of York in the twist'. All light infantry regiments wore the bugle-horn badge in one shape or another. Only the Oxfordshire and Buckinghamshire Light Infantry, as the original light infantry, wore a simple bugle-horn. The badges of all the others were differenced in various ways, as reference to the badges at the head of appropriate sections in this book will show.

In 1881 the 51st was linked to the 105th Madras Light Infantry, which had been raised in 1839 as the 2nd Madras (European Light Infantry) Regiment in the East India Company's service. It was taken into the British army in 1861.

The Regiment wore blue facings and marched to *With Jockey to the Fair*. The museum is in Doncaster Museum and Art Gallery, Chequer Road, and the Colours and memorials are in the Regimental Chapel in York Minster. On 10th July 1969, the 165th anniversary of the establishment of Sir John Moore's Light Brigade, the Regiment became the 2nd Battalion, The Light Infantry.

Minden, Corunna, Fuentes d'Onor, Salamanca, Vittoria, Pyrenees, Nivelle, Orthes, Peninsula, Waterloo, Pegu, Ali Masjid, Afghanistan 1878-80, Burma 1885-7, Modder River, South Africa 1899-1902.

Le Cateau, Marne 1914 '18, Messines 1914 '15 '18, Ypres 1914 '15 '17 '18, Somme 1916 '18, Cambria 1917 '18, Havrincourt, Sambre, Italy 1917-18, Macedonia 1915-17.

Norway 1940, Fontenoy le Pesnil, North West Europe 1944-5, Argoub Sellah, Sicily 1943, Salerno, Minturno, Anzio, Gemmano Ridge, Burma 1942.

THE YORK AND LANCASTER REGIMENT

65th Foot raised in 1756.
Became the 2nd Yorkshire,
North Riding, Regt in 1782.
84th Foot raised in 1794.
Became the York and Lancaster
Regt in 1809.

The title of the Regiment was derived from the Duchies of York and Lancaster, not the cities. A large part of the Duchy of Lancaster lies within the county of Yorkshire, so that this was clearly a Yorkshire regiment. Its recruiting area was that part of the West Riding which lies around Sheffield, Rotherham and Barnsley—Hallamshire. (The 4th Territorial Battalion was in fact officially known as the Hallamshires).

In 1940 the 1st Battalion was carried to Norway on the cruiser *Sheffield*, and she brought back the survivors of that disastrous campaign. A close association was maintained afterwards with the ship and in 1943 the Regiment received the Freedom of the City of Sheffield, which had already adopted the ship.

The badge was the ducal coronet and united rose (the 84th's badge) and the royal tiger awarded to the 65th for over twenty years' distinguished service in India. The two regiments were linked in 1881. The new regiment wore white facings, and the 1st Battalion marched to *The Jockey of York*, the 2nd to *The York and Lancaster*.

In 1968, as the junior regiment of the King's Division, it was disbanded. The principal lodging place of the Colours and memorials is Sheffield Cathedral, with others in York Minster, Ranmoor church in Sheffield, the parish churches of Barnsley, Pontefract and Rotherham, and St. Mary's church, Dover. The museum is in the Brian O'Malley Library and Arts Centre, Walker Place, Rotherham.

Guadaloupe 1759, Martinique 1794, India 1796-1819, Nive, Peninsula, Arabia, New Zealand, Lucknow, Tel-el-Kebir, Egypt 1882-84, Relief of Ladysmith, South Africa 1899-1902,

Ypres 1915 '17 '18, Somme 1916 '18, Messines 1917 '18, Passchendaele, Cambrai 1917 '18, Lys, Selle, Piave, Macedonia 1915-18, Gallipoli 1915.

Fontenoy le Pesnil, Antwerp-Turnhout Canal, Tobruk 1941, Mine de Sedjenane, Sicily 1943, Salerno, Minturno, Crete, North Arakan, Chindits 1944.

LIST OF BATTLE HONOURS

Colours commemorate great actions in the past history of the Regiment. They do not represent a complete guide to a regiment's history, for it might have taken part in an action or service for which no battle honour was awarded. Another complication is that so many honours were won in the World Wars, that they could not all be placed on the Colours.

Regiments were therefore allowed to select 10 honours for the First World War, and 10 for the Second, to be placed on the Queen's Colour. Others are placed on the Regimental Colour. In this list 'Germans' is abbreviated to 'G', and 'Japanese' to 'J'.

Aam *1944 v. G., Holland.*
Abyssinia *1868 v. Ethiopians.*
　　　　1941 v. Italians.
Abu Klea *1885 v. tribesmen, Sudan.*
Afghanistan *1839-42 v. Persians and Afghans.*
　　　　1878-80 v. Afghans.
　　　　1919 v. Afghans.
Ahmed Khel *1880 v. Afghans.*
Aisne *1914-18 v. G., France.*
Akarit *1943 v. G. and Italians, Tunis.*
Alam el Halfa *1942 v. G. and Italians, Egypt.*
Albert *1916 '18 v. G., France.*
Albuhera *1811 v. French, Spain.*
Alem Hamza *1942 v. G. and Italians, Libya.*
Ali Masjid *1878 v. Afghans.*
Aliwal *1846 v. Sikhs, India.*
Aller *1945 v. G., Germany.*
Ally Ghur *1803 v. Mahrattas, India.*
Alma *1854 v. Russians, Crimea.*
Amiens *1918 v. G., France.*
Ancre *1916 '18 v. G., France.*
Antwerp *1944 v. G., Belgium.*
Anzio *1944 v. G., Italy.*
Arabia *1809. 1819 v. pirates.*
Aradoura *1944 v. J., Assam.*
Argenta Gap *1944 v. G., Italy.*
Armentieres *1914 v. G., France.*
Arnhem *1944 v. G., Holland.*
Arras *1917, '18, '40 v. G., France.*
Arroyos dos Molinos *1811 v. French, Spain.*
Atbara *1898 v. tribesmen, Sudan.*
Athens *1944 v. Communist rebels, Greece.*
Ava *1825 v. Burmese, Burma.*
Badajoz *1812 v. French, Spain.*
Baghdad *1917 v. Turks, Mesopotamia.*
Baluchistan *1918 v. tribesmen, India.*
Bapaume *1918 v. G., France.*
Barrosa *1810 v. French, Spain.*
Batu Pahat *1942 v. J., Malaya.*
Bazentin *1916 v. G., France.*
Belhamed *1941 v. G. and Italians, Libya.*
Belleisle *1761 v. French, Atlantic.*
Bhurtpore *1805 v. Mahrattas, India.*
Bladensburg *1814 v. Americans, U.S.A.*
Blenheim *1704 v. French and Bavarians, Germany.*
Bligny *1918 v. G., France.*
Bois de Buttes *1918 v. G., France.*
Bourguebus Ridge *1944 v. G. France.*
Bremen *1945 v. G., Germany.*
Brinkum *1945 v. G., Germany.*

Brieux Bridgehead *1944 v. G., France.*
Burma *1885-7 v. Burmese.*
　　　1942-5 v. J.
Busaco *1810 v. French, Spain.*
Bushire *1808 v. native princes, India.*
Caen *1944 v. G., France.*
Cambrai *1917 '18 v. G., France.*
Campoleone *1944 v. G., Italy.*
Cape of Good Hope *1806 v. Dutch, S. Africa.*
Cassel *1940 v. G., France.*
Cassino *1944 v. G., Italy.*
Canton *1857 v. Chinese, China.*
Cauldron *1942 v. G. and Italians, Libya.*
Central India *1858 v. mutineers.*
Centuripe *1943 v. G. and Italians, Sicily.*
Chillianwallah *1849 v. Sikhs, India.*
Chindits *1942-4 v. J., Burma.*
Chitral *1895 v. tribesmen, N.W. Frontier, India.*
Cleve *1945 v. G., Germany.*
Copenhagen *1801 v. Danes, Denmark.*
Coriano *1944 v. G., Italy.*
Corunna *1809 v. French, Spain.*
Cosina Canal Crossing *1944 v. G., Italy.*
Courtrai *1918 v. G., Belgium.*
Crete *1941 v. G.*
Csestiphon *1915 v. Turks, Mesopotamia.*
Cuidad Rodrigo *1812 v. French, Spain.*
Damiano *1944 v. G., Italy.*
Deig *1780: 1804 v. Mahrattas, India.*
Delhi *1803 v. Mahrattas, India.*
　　1857 v. mutineers.
Dettingen *1743 v. French, Germany.*
Djebel bou Aoukaz *1943 v. G., Tunis.*
Djebel Kesskiss *1943 v. G., N. Africa.*
Doiran *1917 '18 v. Bulgars, Macedonia.*
Dominica *1761 v. French, West Indies.*
Dunkirk *1940 v. G., France.*
Duoro *1809 v. French, Portugal.*
Dyle *1940 v. G., Belgium.*
Egmont-op-Zee *1799 v. French and Dutch, Holland.*
Egypt *1801 v. French.*
　　1882 v. Egyptian rebels.
　　1884 v. tribesmen in Sudan.
　　1916 v. Turks.
El Alamein *1942 v. G. and Italians, Egypt.*
El Mughar *1917 v. Turks, Palestine.*

54

Enfidaville *1943 v. G. and Italians, Tunis.*
Epehy *1918 v. G., France.*
Escaut *1940 v. G., France.*
Falaise *1944 v. G., France.*
Feisote *1944 v. G., Italy.*
Ferozeshah *1845 v. Sikhs, India.*
Festubert *1915 v. G., France.*
Fontenoy le Pesnil *1944 v. G., France.*
Forli *1945 v. G., Italy.*
Fort Dufferin *1945 v. J., Burma.*
France and Flanders *1914-18 v. G.*
Frezenburg *1915 v. G., Belgium.*
Fuentes d'Onoro *1811 v. French, Spain.*
Gallipoli *1915-16 v. Turks, Turkey.*
Gargliano Crossing *1943 v. G., Italy.*
Gaza *1917 v. Turks, Palestine.*
Gazala *1942 v. G. and Italians, Libya.*
Geilenkirchen *1944 v. G., Germany.*
Gemmano Ridge *1944 v. G., Italy.*
Gheluvelt *1914 v. G., Belgium.*
Ghuznee *1839 v. Afghans.*
Gibraltar *1704-5, 1778-83 v. Spaniards.*
Givenchy *1914 v. G., France.*
Goch *1945 v. G., Germany.*
Goojerat *1849 v. Sikhs and Afghans, India.*
Gothic Line *1944 v. G., Italy.*
Guadaloupe *1759, 1810 v. French, West Indies.*
Gueriat El Aatch *1943 v. G., North Africa.*
Habbaniya *1941 v. rebels, Iraq.*
Hafir *1896 v. tribesmen, Sudan.*
Havannah *1762 v. Spaniards, West Indies.*
Havrincourt *1918 v. G., France.*
Helles *1915 v. Turks, Gallipoli.*
Hill 60 *1915 etc v. G., Belgium.*
Hill 112 *1944 v. G., France.*
Hindenburg Line *1918 v. G., France.*
Hindoostan *late C.18th, India.*
Hochwald *1945 v. G., Italy.*
Hong Kong *1941 v. J., China.*
Hooge *1915 v. G., Belgium.*
Hook *1953 v. Chinese, Korea.*
Hunts Gap *1943 v. G., Tunis.*
Hyderabad *1843 v. Moslems, India.*
Italy *1917-8 v. G. and Austrians. 1943-5 v. G.*
Imjin *1951 v. Chinese, Korea.*
Imphal *1944 v. J., Assam.*
Inkerman *1854 v. Russians, Crimea.*
Jahore *1942 v. J., Malaya.*
Java *1812 v. Dutch.*
Jerusalem *1917 v. Turks, Palestine.*
Kabul *1879 v. Afghans, Afghanistan.*
Kandahar *1880 v. Afghans, Afghanistan.*
Kemmel *1918 v. G., Belgium.*
Keren *1940 v. Italians, Eritrea.*
Khan Baghdadi *1918 v. Turks, Mesopotamia.*
Khartoum *1898 v. tribesmen, Sudan.*
Khelat *1839 v. Afghans, Afghanistan.*
Kilimanjaro *1916 v. G., East Africa.*
Kimberley *1899 v. Boers, South Africa.*
Kirbekan *1885 v. tribesmen, Sudan.*
Kohima *1944 v. J., Assam.*

Koosh-ab *1856 v. Persians, Persia.*
Korea, *1950-3 North Koreans and Chinese.*
Kut al Amara *1916·'17 v. Turks, Mesopotamia.*
La Bassee *1914 v. G., France.*
Ladysmith *1899-1900 v. Boers, South Africa.*
Langemarck *1914 '17 v. G., Belgium.*
Le Cateau *1914 v. G., France*
Leros *1943 v. G., Dodecanese.*
Leswarree *1803 v. Mahrattas, India.*
Longstop Hill *1943 v. G., Tunis.*
Loos *1915 v. G., France.*
Louisburg *1758 v. French, Canada.*
Lucknow *1857 v. mutineers, India.*
Lys *1918 v. G., France.*
Macedonia *1915-18 v. Bulgars.*
Madagascar *1942 v. Vichy French.*
Maharajpore *1843 v. Mahrattas, India.*
Maida *1805 v. French, Italy.*
Malaya *1941-2 v. J.*
Malplaquet *1709 v. French, Low Countries.*
Malta *1941-2 v. G. and Italian air attacks.*
Maltot *1944 v. G., France.*
Mandalay *1945 v. J., Burma.*
Marabout *1801 v. French, Egypt.*
Mareth *1943 v. G. and Italians, Tunis.*
Marne *1914 v. G., France.*
Marradi *1945 v. G., Italy.*
Martinique *1762, 1794, 1809 v. French, West Indies.*
Maungdaw *1942 v. J., Burma.*
Medenine *1943 v. G., North Africa.*
Medjez Plain, *1943 v. G. and Italians, Tunis.*
Meeanee *1843 v. Baluchis, India.*
Meggido *1918 v. Turks, Palestine.*
Meiktila *1945 v. J., Burma.*
Merjayun *1941 v. Vichy French, Syria.*
Mesopotamia *1916-18 v. Turks.*
Messines *1917 '18 v. G., Belgium.*
Minden *1759 v. French, Germany.*
Mine de Sedjenane *1943 v. G., Tunis.*
Minturno *1944 v. G., Italy.*
Modder River *1899 v. Boers, South Africa.*
Mons *1914 v. G., Belgium.*
Monte Cassino *1943 v. G., Italy.*
Monte Ceco *1944 v. G., Italy.*
Monte Gamberaldi *1944 v. G., Italy.*
Monte Grande *1944 v. G., Italy.*
Monte Lamone *1944 v. G., Italy.*
Monte Video *1806 v. Spaniards, South America.*
Mont Pincon *1944 v. G., France.*
Moodkee *1845 v. Sikhs, India.*
Mooltjan *1849 v. Sikhs, India.*
Mozza Grogna *1943 v. G., Italy.*
Myinmu Bridgehead *1945 v. J., Burma.*
Myitson *1945 v. J., Burma.*
Mysore *late C. 18th v. Sultan, India.*
Naktung Bridgehead *1950 v. North Koreans.*
Namur *1695 v. French, Belgium. 1914 v. G., Belgium.*

Nederrijn *1944 v. G., Holland.*
Neuve Chapelle *1915 v. G., France.*
New Zealand *1844, 1860 v. Maoris.*
Ngakyedauk Pass *1944 v. J., Burma.*
Niagara *1812 v. Americans, North America.*
Nile *1884-5 v. tribesmen, Sudan.*
Nive *1813 v. French, France.*
Nivelle *1813 v. French, France.*
Nonne Bosschen *1914 v. G., Belgium.*
Normandy Landing *1944 v. G., France.*
North Africa *1940-3 v. G. and Italians.*
North Arakan *1944 v. J., Burma.*
North West Europe *1940, '44-5 v. G.*
Norway *1940 v. G.*
Nyaungu Bridgehead *1945 v. J., Burma.*

Odon *1944 v. G., France.*
Orthes *1814 v. French, France.*
Oudenarde *1708 v. French, Low Countries.*
Oued Zarga *1943 v. G., Tunis.*
Ourthe *1944-5 v. G., Belgium.*

Paardeberg *1900 v. Boers, South Africa.*
Palestine *1917-18 v. Turks.*
Palmyra *1941 v. Vichy French, Syria.*
Passchendaele *1917 v. G., Belgium.*
Paungde *1942 v. J., Burma.*
Pegu *1852 v. Burmese, Burma.*
Peiwar Kotal *1878 v. Afghans, Afghanistan.*
Pekin *1860 v. Chinese, China.*
Peninsula *1808-14 v. French, Spain.*
Persia *1856-7 v. Persians.*
Piave *1918 v. Austrians, Italy.*
Pilckem *1917 v. G., Belgium.*
Pinwe *1944 v. J., Burma.*
Plassey *1757 v. Bengalese, India.*
Primosole Bridge *1943 v. G. and Italians, Sicily.*
Punjaub *1849 v. Sikhs, India.*
Punniar *1843 v. Maharattas, India.*

Quebec *1759 v. French, Canada.*
Queenstown *1813 v. Americans, North America.*

Ramillies *1706 v. French, Low Countries.*
Regalbuto *1943 v. G., Sicily.*
Reichwald *1945 v. G., Germany.*
Rhine *1945 v. G., Germany.*
Rhineland *1945 v. G., Germany.*
Rimini Line *1944 v. G., Italy.*
Robaa Valley *1943 v. G., Tunis.*
Roer *1945 v. G., Germany.*
Rolica *1808 v. French, Portugal.*
Rome *1944 v. G., Italy.*
Rumari *1916 v. Turks, Egypt.*
St. Julien *1915 v. G., Belgium.*
St. Lucia *1778, 1803 v. French, West Indies.*
St. Omer-la Bassee *1940 v. G., France.*
St. Quentin *1918 v. G., France.*
St. Valery en Caux *1940 v. G., France.*
Salamanca *1812 v. French, Spain.*
Salerno *1943 v. G., Italy.*
Sambre *1918 v. G., France.*

Sangro *1944 v. G., Italy.*
San Sebastian *1812 v. French, Spain.*
Sari Bair *1915 v. Turks, Gallipoli.*
Scheldt *1944 v. G., Belgium.*
Scinde *1843 v. Moslem states, India.*
Seine *1944 v. G., France.*
Selle *1918 v. G., France.*
Seringapatam *1799 v. Sultan of Mysore, India.*
Sevastopol *1855 v. Russians, Crimea.*
Shaiba *1915 v. Turks, Mesopotamia.*
Sharqat *1918 v. Turks, Mesopotamia.*
Shweli *1945 v. J., Burma.*
Sicily *1943 v. Italians and G.*
Sidi Barrani *1940 v. Italians, Egypt.*
Singapore Island *1942 v. J., Malaya.*
Sittang *1942 v. J., Burma.*
Sobraon *1846 v. Sikhs, India.*
Somme *1916 '18 v. G., France.*
Souleuvre *1944 v. G., France.*
South Africa *1846-7, 1851-3, 1879-81 v. tribesmen.*
　　　　　　1899-1902 v. Boers.
Struma *1917 v. Bulgars, Macedonia.*
Suakin *1885 v. tribesmen, Sudan.*
Surinam *1804 v. Dutch, South America.*
Suvla *1915 v. Turks, Gallipoli.*

Taku Forts *1860 v. Chinese, China.*
Talavera *1809 v. French, Spain.*
Tangier *1662-80 v. Moors, Morocco.*
Tarifa *1812 v. French, Spain.*
Taukkyan *1942 v. J., Burma.*
Tebourba Gap *1943 v. G. and Italians, Tunis.*
Tel-el-Kebir *1882 v. rebels, Egypt.*
Tell' Asur *1917 v. Turks, Palestine.*
Tigris *1916 v. Turks, Mesopotamia.*
Tilly-sur-Seuilles *1944 v. G., France.*
Tirah *1897-8 v. tribesmen, N.W. Frontier, India.*
Tobruk *1940-3 v. G. and Italians, Libya.*
Tofrek *1885 v. tribesmen, Sudan.*
Tournai *1709 v. French, Low Countries.*
Tournhout Canal *1944 v. G., Belgium.*
Trasimene Line *1944 v. G., Italy.*
Trigno *1943 v. G., Italy.*
Tunis *1943 v. G. and Italians.*

Valenciennes *1918 v. G., France.*
Venrail *1944 v. G., Holland.*
Villers Bretonneux *1918 v. G., France.*
Villiers Bocage *1944 v. G., France.*
Vimiera *1808 v. French, Portugal.*
Vimy *1917 v. G., France.*
Vittoria *1813 v. French, Spain.*
Vittorio Veneto *1918 v. Austrians, Italy.*

Waterloo *1815 v. French, Belgium.*
Weeze *1945 v. G., Germany.*
Wilhelmstahl *1758 v. French, Low Countries.*
Wormhoudt *1940 v. G., Belgium.*

Yenangyaung *1942 v. J., Burma.*
Ypres *1914 '15 '17 v. G., Belgium.*
Ypres-Commines Canal *1940 v. G., Belgium.*
Yu *1944 v. J., Burma.*

Zetten *1945 v. G., Holland.*

Printed by C. I. Thomas & Sons Ltd, Haverfordwest